S0-CFK-011

LET THE PSALMS SPEAK

LET THE PSALMS SPEAK

BY CHARLES L. TAYLOR

GREENWICH

CONNECTICUT

1961

Library of Congress Catalog Card Number: 61-11313
Design by Stefan Salter
363-761-C-4

Printed in the United States of America

PREFACE

In the days of President Remsen B. Ogilby, whose capacity for fun-making was boundless, two men gave a table to Trinity College, Hartford, on which he suggested that they put an inscription from Psalm 55:15. In the Prayer Book Psalter this reads, "We took sweet counsel together and walked in the house of God as friends." As the donors turned to their King James Bibles, however, they read, "Let death seize upon them, and let them go down quick into hell, for wickedness is in their dwellings and among them."

The problems which the Psalms present are much more numerous than any difference in numbering. In the verse just mentioned, should *hell,* with all its connotations of days long after the psalmists, be employed to translate the word *Sheol? Quick* means *alive,* not *rapid.* Why use archaic language? But, more pertinently still, have Christians today any real justification for using this type of imprecation at all?

We suspect that many of us use the Psalms without a clear idea of what they mean, and that others would like to know the Psalms better but are perplexed as to where to begin. The toughest-minded among us find in some parts of the Psalter meat, in other parts bone, but which are which? The faithful read psalms day after day, week after week, in private or public worship, but in their love of cadences or the beauty of words, such as "we took sweet counsel together and walked in the house of God as friends," perhaps grow deaf to what they profoundly say. Some who have never heard the Psalms may possibly welcome a hearing aid. At least the attempt should constantly be made to render those songs of Zion intelligible in a world very different and yet very like the world into which they were born, for the scene may be a "strange land," but people are still plagued by the age-old problems common to man, and the Lord no less is "a great King above all gods."

This book is one such attempt. When the invitation came to deliver the Kellogg Lectures for 1960 at the Episcopal Theological School, Cambridge, Massachusetts, I welcomed this opportunity to wrestle with the difficulty caused by the differences between the psalmists' period and ours. Some of the substance of this book I had already given in Lowell Lectures at King's Chapel, Boston, in Birks Lectures at McGill University, Montreal, and at the United Theological Seminary, Dayton. In the interests of allowing the Psalms to speak as clearly as possible I have felt free to make my own translations; sometimes I have followed the Revised Standard or King James version, sometimes that of the Prayer Book. The reader advised beforehand will not be confused either by this fact or by the differences in verse numbering. If this book is less detailed and documented than some desire, that is due to its practical aim. Indebtedness to many students of the Psalms will readily be apparent to scholars, even when no specific credit is given.

To all who have made this book possible, I extend my thanks, to Dean Coburn and the Faculty of the Episcopal Theological School; to the typists, especially Miss Beatrice M. Hamilton and Mrs. Robert J. Thompson; to my colleague, Dr. Jesse H. Ziegler and to another source of never failing encouragement, the Dean of Liverpool (Dr. F. W. Dillistone); to Mr. Arthur R. Buckley of The Seabury Press; and not least to a very patient wife.

Who is adequate to the task of helping the Psalms come alive among us? Nobody possesses all the skills required, yet each of us has his part—a worshipping part, an understanding part, and a communicating part. In the spirit of the inscription over the gate of Marischal College, Aberdeen, "They have said. What say they? Let them say."

C. L. T.

CONTENTS

LET THE PSALMS SPEAK

I.

THE PERMANENCE OF THE PSALMISTS' EXPERIENCES

Along one wall of the very beautiful chapel at the Kirchliche Hochschule in Berlin is a sculptured representation of man's history from Adam to John the Baptist. Noah is there, Elijah, Job also, and others, but because of a miscalculation of the available space, David is out of sight, around the corner. Just as he is absent from that wall, have the poems that bear his name lost their position in the services of the Church? The divine artist seems to have planned to assist man's worship through the Psalms; but today we wonder how to use them, where to place them.

The Psalms in a New Age

To fall back on the platitude of platitudes: we live in a different world. Our nation, so they tell us, "in many measurable respects is the most successful civilization that ever existed." [1] We are the wealthiest people in history. On the other hand, the Psalms—at least some ninety of them—reflect misery in one form or another, poverty, sickness, persecution, war, or the danger of imminent death; they were written "out of the depths." Therefore the tongue of an honest and thoughtful man today may stick when he starts to read a psalm that begins:

Bow down thine ear, O Lord, and hear me;
  for I am poor, and in misery.
Preserve thou my soul, for I am holy . . .

O God, the proud are risen against me;
  And the congregations of violent men have sought
  after my soul. (*Ps. 86:1, 2, and 14 BCP*)

He is not poor nor miserable, and certainly not holy; and he hopes that he is not deluded by a persecution complex.

Ultimately we shall argue for the continuity of man's basic experiences, but we are fools if we close our eyes to the discontinuity of our time with time past. It is impossible to speak of the Psalms now as we did even ten years ago. If we have read Galbraith's *Affluent Society* or Riesman's *Lonely Crowd,* or a host of other books like *The Organization Man, The Hidden Persuaders, The Status Seekers,* or *The Ugly American,* we can hardly avoid the question: how are we to sing the Lord's songs in a strange land? For the problem is not only a matter of modern affluence. It is not only that the advances in technology of the past five or six decades have been greater than those recorded in history up until this century began; or that the past twenty years have seen more scientific discoveries than any prior forty; or that both urban life and rural life have changed so vastly in twenty years, to say nothing of the developments over the decades immediately preceding. It is also that to thousands who have stood partly within the Christian tradition, the foundations of that tradition seem to be destroyed and they ask, "What can the righteous do?" (Ps. 11:3), while for millions of others the tradition-directed society is a phenomenon so far in the past that the Psalms hardly enter their consciousness as words having meaning. And this despite the so-called success of the churches, the vague interest in religion or the superficial quest for religious authority.

Our first question, then, is whether the experiences of two thousand years ago can also be ours. But even if this question is answered affirmatively, there is a second which is intimately connected with it: how far do the images in the Psalms correspond now to the experiences symbolized? A figure such as "The Lord is my shepherd" (Ps. 23:1), which adequately expressed the conviction of a pastoral society, may be quite without meaning to someone dwelling in a city slum. One hundred years ago Abraham Lincoln might have been able to say about the Psalms: "They are the best, for I find in them something for every day in the week."[2] But is not the difference between 1960 and 1860 greater than the difference between A.D. 1860 and 260 B.C.? What if even Lincoln's thought forms are obsolete? On the one hand is our obligation to be honest, to use words which accurately express experience. On the other, is the realization that words or other symbols are also the means by which we are led into experiences hitherto unknown.

Indeed, some of the psalmists' figures of speech are, and must be, alien to us, for example, the pelican in the wilderness or the bottle in the smoke under the roof of a one-room house. As Christians, we also hesitate to evoke certain attitudes or emotions found in the Psalms: "Consume them in thy wrath, consume them, that they may perish." (Ps. 59:13 BCP) "O God, break the teeth in their mouths. . . . Let them vanish like water that runs away. . . . Let them be like the snail which dissolves into slime, like the untimely birth that never sees the sun. . . . The righteous will rejoice when he sees the vengeance; he will bathe his feet in the blood of the wicked." (Ps. 58:6-10 RSV)

Yet the psalmist's imagery, although at first foreign to us, may, after some thought, be the means by which we are led to a conscious realization of what we only vaguely felt or thought before; at other times it may be the means of a new experience. In Psalm 103, for example, we find this statement:

> As the heavens form a canopy over the earth,
> his devotion spreads over his worshippers.
> (*Ps. 103:11*)

Scientifically this statement may be challenged; nevertheless, both for Jew and Christian, it contains no less truth than does the precise mathematical formula developed in the laboratory.

Or consider the picture of creation in Psalm 104, where God, after laying the immovable foundations of the earth, covered it with water as with a garment, then commanded that water to flow up and down, up to the skies, down to the seas and to the underground places appointed for them from which they bubble up in springs. Behind the strangeness of this description lie the great affirmations: God is exceeding glorious, he created this world, the winds and the fire are his servants, it is he who brings food out of the earth, wine that makes glad the heart of man, and oil to make him a cheerful countenance. Under God's appointment of night and day, man goes forth to his work and to his labor until the evening. Land and sea creatures wait all upon him that he may give them food in due season. When he takes away their breath, they die, and are turned again to their dust; when he lets his spirit go forth, he renews the face of the earth.

No summary paraphrase can do this psalm justice. Its word images may help a man to begin to appreciate nature even before his actual encounter with nature itself. Just as a child is taught to express his thanks to his hostess at a party long before he actually feels deep gratitude and so is helped to grow into the experience, so these symbols are among the most precious we know in helping us to comprehend that the glorious majesty of the Lord shall endure forever, that the Lord rejoices in his works, and that our proper response is to sing unto the Lord as long as we live.

Here then is our dilemma. Because of the vast changes in the modern world, some question the value of this ancient poetry we call the Psalter. The Church, they argue, "cannot train her clergy for a medieval or nineteenth-century way of life and ministry," [3]—a training of which the recitation of the Psalter in its entirety each month was an integral part. The regard in which the Psalms were held formerly has vanished; and we cannot recall it. Now it would be untrue to insist that a man cannot understand life unless he be thoroughly versed in this literature. Not everyone must learn its language. God willing, we shall not make excessive claims for the Psalter. But those who have lived with this poetry for many a year are convinced of its power to quicken the imagination, to deepen insights, to kindle affection, to strengthen the will—in short, to increase a man's hold on life. If the Psalter is abandoned today, we shall be traitors not only to a generation of God's children,[4] but to ourselves.

Meanwhile our inheritance bids us be ill-content with a comfortable community of our own, even a worshipping community, and summons us to bring the world to the knowledge and love and service of God. We do not study the Psalms for our private satisfaction. Perhaps the priest and the Levite in the parable of the Good Samaritan were reading their Psalter as they passed by on the other side. We shall not, therefore, boast over this literature, nor even defend it, but rather seek to illuminate it. Let it speak for itself. Sometimes using traditional language, sometimes a modern idiom, we venture to search out what its authors meant, what experiences lay behind their words, and how, in their idiom, they were speaking to the life of our time. Through this Psalter we, too, have known that which we dare not, and will not, deny, and to which we bear witness.

Questions Then and Now

One way of comparing the ancient world with the modern is to juxtapose the questions each asks. No one of us could easily gather into a short paragraph all the complexity of the modern mood. But any of us can analyze a few of the sources of troubles and uneasiness in our never-so-successful civilization: Is the danger of another war really lessening, or are we closer and closer to the time when some blundering idiot will blow and burn us all to bits? Where is there true security? Will the current explosion of population mean a vast increase in the world's misery through poverty and strife and forms of death worse than those caused by familiar diseases? Will the incidence of mental illness, for example, multiply until it will be difficult to distinguish the sane from the insane? Why are there today so many neurotics—one in ten mentally or emotionally sick—and why in this age of plenty so many suicides? Is it because man has lost his bearings, lost a sense of why he is alive, and with that suffered the further loss of what he is called to do and whither he shall tend?

Because contemporary man's charts and compass have gone over the rail, what wonder that there is mutiny on shipboard, emotional drives warring against reason, and reason abdicating responsibility in favor of medical aid.

> All hail, convenient Ego,
> Accommodating Id!
> You are the fundamental cause
> Of all behaviour that the laws
> Of God and man forbid.
> Whenever we are mean or gross,
> It's just our Ea and our Nos;
> So let us sing this helpful song—
> 'There's no such thing as right or wrong.
> It's nothing but the Ego,
> The Ego and the Id.' [5]

But despite all such "helpful songs," and our whistling to keep courage up, men still lead, in this day, lives that lack fulfillment, or perhaps are more than ever unfulfilled. Some have feelings of loneliness, of not being wanted; some on a low, selfish plane increase their greed and their wealth, but not their contentment; others on a higher plane feel acutely the world's injustice and wonder how ever the world's increasing ills are to be cured. Always there is the problem how to be in right relation with one's fellow man, in home, in business, in church, in nation; and for most people, if not all, there is the encounter with suffering, pain, loneliness, unfulfilled desire, the guilt of past mistakes, and the tragedy of hopes and purposes unrealized. Many a man does not know who he is, whence his origin, what he is on earth to be and do, how to deal with trouble, how to meet and trust his neighbor, whither he is bound, how to live so that this haunting sense of capacities unrealized may be overcome, and then how to die.

Like the dancers around the fire, of whom the late Donald Baillie wrote,[6] we wonder why the rhythm is so upset; why we are faced away from the light; why we are afraid of our own shadows; why we stumble over our own and our brother's feet; why all is confusion and dread rather than light and harmony and joy and peace. Who will turn us around?

If now we turn to the Psalms to see what questions they raise, it is clear that the basic perplexities are not essentially different. It is instructive to examine the words that immediately precede the one hundred or so question marks in the Psalter. Here is the timeless query, "What is man?" (Ps. 8:4) Then as now, "Whence cometh my help?" (Ps. 121:1) and again, what happens after this life: "Will the dust praise thee?" (Ps. 30:9) "Dost thou work wonders for the dead?" (Ps. 88:10) No age escapes these questions.

Most of them fall into four categories: (a) The ethical question—what is right? "Who shall ascend the hill of the Lord?" (Ps. 24:3) "Who shall sojourn in thy tent?" (Ps. 15:1) "How can a young man keep his way pure?" (Ps. 119:9) (b) The polemic question—why, given the justice of God, do nations conspire (Ps. 2:1) tyrants boast (Ps.

52:1), the wicked exult (Ps. 94:3), and fools continue in their folly (Ps. 14:1-4)? Since wrong *ipso facto* must be futile, "Fools, when will you be wise? Does the one who made the ear not hear, or the creator of the eye not see?" (Ps. 94:9) Can you not understand that pride must lead to destruction for those who say, "Our lips are ours, who is our master?" (Ps. 12:4) for "Who is God, but the Lord?" (Ps. 18:31) (c) The philosophical question which the psalmist, often using the third person, asks of the God without, although he knows he should not fear what any man can do to him (Ps. 118:6). "Why does God stand afar off and hide?" (Ps. 10:1) Will he spurn forever? (Ps. 77:7) How long will he be angry with his people's prayers? (Ps. 80:4) Why does God seem to sleep and hide his face and forget? (Ps. 44:23) Why should the nations cast into the teeth of his people, "Where is now thy God?" (Pss. 115:2; 42:3, 10) how long? is it always? (Ps. 13:1) and (d) The religious question which the psalmist asks of the God within—what is the meaning of all my trouble and all my striving? *Eli, Eli, lama sabachthani?* (Ps. 22:1) Why must I die? To what good end do I live? What is my hope? These doubts he counters with questions in another vein: "And now, Lord, for what do I wait? My hope is in thee." (Ps. 39:7) "Whom have I but thee?" (Ps. 73:25) Therefore why should I fear in times of trouble? (Ps. 49:5) With the Lord for my light, my aid, the stronghold of my life, of whom shall I be afraid? (Ps. 27:1) What shall I render to the Lord for all his bounty to me? (Ps. 116:12) why be cast down and why murmur within? (Ps. 43:5) Thus, in the end, the psalmist's knowledge of what God has done for him in the past sustains him in the present and gives him confidence for the future.

We now propose to explore the psalmists' answer to these questions and to study the underlying experiences behind their words, for both the questions and the experiences still perplex our world.

The Ethical Question

First, let us examine the ethical question as it is set forth in Psalm 50. While the text has suffered considerable alteration and supplementation, including an editorial effort to divide the psalm into two parts addressed respectively to saints and sinners, the basic pattern remains clear. There were once probably twenty lines: four of introduction; then eight about man's duty to God, a duty of devotion without any need for futile sacrifices; and then eight about duty to one's neighbor, a duty which is performed through the keeping of God's commandments.

What are the essential experiences here? Let us recognize at once that while this is not one of the most profound psalms, it does show its author struggling to escape, like St. Paul, from a body caught in the clutches of sin, and it does offer important clues to freedom. (1) The first truth is that the God who offers his saving help is also a God who demands. Without his concern for justice the Lord would be a puny God. (2) Moreover, God's justice is rooted in the constitution of the universe; this is an affair of the whole earth and the heavens too. (3) Once more, the fact that Israel is his people does not exempt them from his requirements; in fact it makes them particularly responsible to observe them. As Amos put it, "You only have I chosen, *therefore* I punish you."

> The Lord speaks and calls the earth
>   from utmost east to utmost west . . .
> He calls to the heavens above
>   and to the earth, to judge his people. . . .
> Hear, my people, and let me speak,
>   Israel, let me testify against you.

(4) Then in the second section of the poem follows the insight that God is not greedy for himself, but that his demand is another aspect of his self-giving. Here appears one of the classic protests from within Judaism itself of the practice of animal sacrifice.

> Not for your sacrifices do I reprove you
>   Nor for your offerings before me continually.
> I will take no yearling from your house
>   Nor he-goats from your folds.
> For mine are all the beasts of the forest,
>   the cattle on a thousand mountains.
> I know all the birds of the heights
>   and the creatures that move in the fields are mine.

If I were hungry, I would not tell you,
  for mine is the world and everything in it.
Should I eat the flesh of bulls
  or drink the blood of goats?

These are no light words, that the world is the Lord's and everything in it, but the psalmist does not stop with a negative rebuke of animal sacrifice. (5) He states positively what God wants—thanksgiving and obedience and the devotion of humble trust:

> Make thanksgiving your sacrifice to the Lord,
>   and perform your vows to the most High,
> and call on me on the day of trouble,
>   let me save you that you may honor me.[7]

This is the experience of God's demand represented in the Catechism: "My duty towards God is to worship him, to give him thanks, to put my whole trust in him, to call upon him." In our prosperity have we forgotten that obligation and promise are both part of God's word, and in the very nature of the universe?

(6) Out of this right relationship to God springs just dealing with one's fellow man. The accusation in the last part of the psalm is that although the accused profess allegiance to God's covenant, in reality they reject it. They forget that God is concerned with the commandments as they bear upon man's duty to man: the eighth commandment which relates to stealing, the seventh to adultery, and

especially the ninth to false witness. They forget the connection between ethics and true piety. Responsibility to God is the only secure source of man's order.

> What right have you to recite my statutes
> or take my covenant on your lips,
> While you hate discipline
> and cast my words behind you?
> When you see a thief, you are happy with him,
> and with adulterers you keep company.
> You unleash your mouth with vile talk
> and your tongue frames deceit.
> You speak shamefully against your brother,
> You slander your mother's son.
> These things have you done while I kept silent,
> You thought that I am like yourself.

(7) Notice the reference to man's perennial attempt to make God in man's image and (8) once more, in the final summary, the truth that the way to honor God is through grateful trust in God and blameless character in dealing with men. The pure in heart are promised, if not the vision of God, the revelation of God's work.

> He who makes thanksgiving his sacrifice honors me
> and the upright in life I will show my saving help.

There are problems in this psalm which we leave to one side, for our aim is to discover what the author knows about the nature of reality, especially as he seeks to discern what is right. Moral obedience is fundamental. "Unless your righteousness exceeds that of the scribes and Pharisees, you will never enter the Kingdom of heaven." (Matt. 5:20) But to exceed means first to include. In a time of religious fervor but ethical indifference, we may well ask if our conduct may be said to reach even this level.

The Polemical Question

The polemical questions in the Psalms are addressed usually to the psalmist's enemies: why be such fools as to deny God's judgment of the nations? There is a relatively little known psalm, the 82nd, which is by no means so difficult as it at first appears. It is a word of encouragement to the people of God in the form of a warning to the proud rulers of the oppressing nations. The rulers are addressed, half-ironically and half-seriously in the fashion current among those nations, as gods. Essentially the truth is that of Ezekiel, "Because thine heart is lifted up, and thou hast said, I am a God, I sit in the seat of God in the midst of the seas; yet thou art man and not God" (Ez. 28:2)—therefore comes death and destruction and the overthrow of all your recognized and considerable wisdom.

> The Lord takes his stand in the divine assembly,
> holding judgment in the midst of the gods.

(1) God's judgment is inescapable, even for kings and those who pretend themselves divine. All authority is held

in trust under him, although neither the political nor ecclesiastical world has yet learned that. (2) Notice also the basis of his judgment, not arbitrary power, but justice and assistance to the helpless. These are the criteria by which those in authority are sifted. The purpose of government is to promote those divine standards, not to disregard them.

> How long will you judge unjustly
> and show partiality to the wicked?
> Give justice for the oppressed and fatherless,
> vindicate the afflicted and destitute.
> Rescue the poor and needy,
> deliver them from the hand of the wicked.

(3) Although these rulers of the nations, as in the Ezekiel passage, seem to be wise, they are foolish: even if they half deceive us into thinking of them more highly than we ought, when God arises, the arrogant or unjust oppressors go the way of other mortal men. The psalmist does not quite say that man's pretension is in itself a cause of his downfall, but he is sure of the downfall.

> They[8] have neither knowledge nor sense,
> walking to and fro in darkness.
> I thought you were divine,
> Sons of the Most High, all of you;
> Nevertheless you shall die like men
> and like any ruler you shall fall.

(4) In faith our author looks forward to the day when the Lord not of one nation, but of all, takes his power and reigns.

> Arise, Lord, judge the earth,
> for to thee belong all the nations.[9]

Are there not profundities of insight and experience here in these brief eight lines which even now our powerful and sophisticated civilization has not really grasped?

The Philosophical Question

We referred earlier to the philosophical question, the psalmists' bewilderment over the seeming remoteness, indifference, and inaction of the good God. The Hebrews of ancient times were not often philosophers; no philosophic answer is given to this so oft repeated plaintive cry, "How long?" The answer is the response of faith, which is not irrational, but firmly rooted in past experience.

Consider for example, Psalm 85, said to have been Cromwell's favorite. The first half reads:

> Once, Lord, thou didst favor thy land,
> thou didst restore the fortunes of Jacob,
> Thou didst forgive the iniquity of thy people,
> thou didst cover all their sin.
> Thou didst withdraw all thy wrath,
> thou didst divert the heat of thy anger.

Restore us again, O God who dost help us,
and withdraw thy indignation against us!
Wilt thou be angry with us forever,
prolonging thy wrath for generations?
Wilt thou not revive us again,
that thy people may rejoice in thee?
Show us, Lord, thy devotion,
and grant us thy deliverance.

Here, first of all, notice the assumption that despite God's present wrath, which the poet hopes will quickly end but which he does not challenge as unjustified, God's favor and help and forgiveness are seen to be his predominant characteristics.[10]

Next is the appeal that God, who has manifested his nature before, will again show himself merciful. Even in the twentieth century, thousands of times every day the prayer rises before him: "O Lord, show thy mercy upon us and grant us thy salvation." His mercy, or loving-kindness, or devotion, or affectionate loyalty, and his salvation, or deliverance, or help are not merely potential; they have been demonstrated. They are a given and a known good. Which nation or individual, prospering even though guilty of great wrongs, could say that God had not "covered" its sin? Notice also the close connection between forgiveness and rejoicing—is one of the reasons for our gloom our guilt?—and further, the nature of salvation or deliverance, which in the latter part of the psalm is connected with glory and more fully described, but here has primary reference to forgiveness. Sin is the obstacle that needs primary attention.

The second half of the psalm begins with the readiness of the psalmist to listen; he has found in his experience that the Lord has something to say. When he speaks, God's word is peace, because his people and his saints or devoted ones who are looking to him find help near. There are certain correspondences between heavenly and earthly realities that give ground for a magnificent hope.

> Let me hear what the Lord speaks.
>   Is it not that he speaks peace
> to his people and to his saints,
>   and to those who turn their hearts to him?
> Surely his help is near his worshippers,
>   that glory may dwell in our land.
> Devotion and faithfulness meet one another,
>   righteousness and peace kiss each other.
> Faithfulness springs up from the earth
>   while righteousness looks down from the sky.
> Moreover the Lord will give prosperity,
>   and our land will yield its increase.
> Righteousness will go before him
>   and peace in the path for his feet.

God's help is at hand; his glory, or the brightness of his presence, may still be known upon earth. His devotion comes out to meet man's faithfulness. His "setting things to rights" is followed by the end of want and war; or turned around, man's loyalty on earth rises to meet the saving, helping, health-producing power that descends from heaven.

Is this pipe dreaming? pretty poetry? or is the best on earth responding to eternal reality? Is this imprecise biblical diction, or are such words as "devotion," "righteousness," "faithfulness," and "peace" capable of ever renewed significance and wider application? [11]

Will the symbols of these visions lay hold on us and on our fellows? If not, who will translate them, for still the world longs for deliverance?

Doubt

There are numerous psalms, some of the best of which we shall come to later, which reveal the psalmists' wrestling, in the depths of his own being, for the hope and the confidence which we too seek. Even in an age of outward prosperity, we wonder whether or not life is only a vain show and whether what we do here will endure. In his *Essays in Liberality,*[12] Canon Vidler has so strikingly expressed much of what we have been trying to say that we incorporate his insights as we speak of Psalm 90.

He points out first the importance of prayer as a road to understanding biblical theology. In general the Psalms begin with an appeal to God, or end there; and it is in this prayerful meeting that the truth is known.

Next he recalls the psalms' declaration of the eternity of

God: from everlasting to everlasting, before the mountains were born, throughout all generations, stands God, in whose sight a thousand years are as yesterday. "At the back of history, both undergirding it and overarching it, is the Eternal, the Lord God. There is a dwelling place for man in history despite the apparent homelessness, the terrible restlessness, the hopeless lack of stability, in historical existence."

Then follow the transitoriness and the sin of man, his double frailty. He is dust, as ephemeral as the grass which sprouts and withers the same day, and he recognizes also that:

> Thou dost set our iniquities before thee,
> our secret sins in the light of thy countenance.
> All our days perish under thy wrath,
> our years are exhausted like a sigh . . .
> And their span is toil and trouble
> for they quickly pass and we fly away.

"In the end history doesn't seem to add up to anything. . . . Up to a point or over certain stretches we can put up what looks like a pretty good show in history but at the heart of it is guilt, the guilt of pride, the guilty secret of historic existence."

"This will strike our sanguine contemporaries as melancholy, but how much profounder it is than the shallow idealism of modern man who is unable or afraid to look into the dark interior of history. It is the eternal holiness of God that makes us sad about our transitoriness and our guilt." "A sense of man's misery is tied to a sense of God's majesty. Modern man has lost both: we as modern men have lost both."

But the pessimism of this psalm, as of the Bible generally, is not of a kind to make us sentimental or morbid, but rather to prompt right action, as we pray:

> "So teach us to count our days,
> that we may secure minds full of wisdom,"

and again that God will return or relent and take pity, and

> "Satisfy us soon with thy devotion
> that we may cry for joy all our days."

When Isaac Watts paraphrased this psalm in "O God, our help in ages past," and used the phrase "our eternal home," he extended the meaning of the psalm to include a hope of immortality; but it was only after the Old Testament period that men deduced that should God allow creatures whom he loved to perish he would deny his own love. Fr. George Tyrrell is very close to the spirit of this psalmist when he calls for a religion free from the "anthropocentric vanity" which exalts man to a false position, a religion providing "an outlook into those immensities in which our greatest philosophers seem less than chirping grasshoppers." [13] For, as Vidler concludes:

> When we have been given that wise grace to come to terms with our transitoriness and our guilt, then no longer is it need-

ful for us to be kept down in the dark by the wrath of God. God can now relent; the morning can come; there are after all open to us glorious satisfactions in history itself; it is possible that we should rejoice now and be glad all our days; but only if God's work appears unto his servants—

> Let thy servants see thee at thy saving work
> and let their children see thy glorious power.

If God is revealed at work within the conditions of our transitoriness, then indeed our existence will be given a sure hope and our guilt will be redeemed. Then indeed we can pray that the work of our hands, what we create in our civilization may be established. . . . We cannot establish it . . . but he can.

At the outset of our discussion we asked ourselves whether the experiences of these psalmists of two thousand or more years ago are also ours. If in exploring these few psalms our answer is negative, let us remember that it is chiefly because our age has lost something precious, not because the psalmists were deficient. Must we not, then, disabuse ourselves of the idea that the study of the Psalms represents a retrogression, an attempt to return to an age that is past? Must we not recognize, rather, that the Psalms call us forward to lands that were explored long ago, but that few of us have visited?

II.

THE PSALMISTS' CONCEPT OF THE TRUTH

We turn now to another problem similar to that of the correspondence of experience, namely, whether the presuppositions underlying the psalmists' thought are sufficiently close to ours to permit us to use this literature without being dishonest. Honesty has a double thrust. It means that so far as possible we should say what we mean and mean what we say, but also that what we mean or what we think should be in correspondence with reality. If we are to be true, as in our heart of hearts we desire to be, then we cannot be content with an integrity which brings us only personal psychological satisfactions, for an idiot can have those; or a kind of social conformity for which our next door neighbors praise us, for the most harmful nationalist or segregationalist can achieve that. Rather we seek for nothing less than an adequate grasp of the sweep of history and a right concept of human destiny and the meaning and purpose of the world. For us who stand in the Jewish-Christian tradition, it is impossible to know the truth, to be honest in the second sense of answering to reality, unless we know the true God who is the beginning and the end of all truth.

Thus the question becomes: do the Psalms lead us to this truth? Specifically: (1) Do they show us man as he is? (2) Do they contain an adequate grasp of the individual's relation to society? (3) How accurate is their concept of history? (4) What do they say about the natural world? and especially, (5) What do they reveal to us about God? Does what they declare of him shed light upon the meaning and purpose of our lives and show us a true hope?

The Truth about Man

What is the truth about man? Any aspect of the plight of modern man one wishes to emphasize is almost certain also to be depicted in the Psalter, whether it be: (a) his lack of identity: "I am a worm and no man" (Ps. 22:6); (b) his estrangement: "I am a stranger with thee, and a sojourner, as all my fathers were" (Ps. 39:14 BCP); (c) his loneliness: "I am like a pelican of the wilderness, I am like an owl of the desert . . . as a sparrow alone on the house top" (Ps. 102:6f. KJV); (d) the emptiness and meaninglessness of his existence: "We spend our years as a tale that is told" (Ps. 90:9 KJV); (e) the fact that his life is corrupted and burdened by his own mistakes: "Mine iniquities are gone over my head, as an heavy burden they are too heavy for me . . . I am bowed down greatly; I go mourning all the day long." (Ps. 38:4, 6 KJV); (f) his feeling of being caught in a net by circumstances beyond his control: "I am for peace, but when I speak, they are for war" (Ps. 120:7); (g) his insecurity in what he so graphically describes as the "miry ooze" (Ps. 40:2); or (h) what the psychologists call his lack of acceptance: "O God, why hast thou cast us off forever?" (Ps. 74:1) The predicament of man is here.

If all this has a contemporary ring, the reason is that it is an honest description of one side of man's nature. He shares with the animals creatureliness, mortality, finitude, and he is even in worse condition than they because he sins as they do not. He is filled with pride; he pretends a power he does not possess; he is vain; he distorts the true picture of himself. These are some of the sources of his misery.

"When I consider thy heavens, the work of thy fingers,
the moon and the stars which thou hast ordained,
What is man, that thou art mindful of him
and the son of man, that thou shouldest notice him?"
(Ps. 8:3f.)

"We bring our years to an end,
as it were a tale that is told." *(Ps. 90:9 BCP)*

"Verily every man living is altogether vanity."
(Ps. 39:6 BCP)

"In my prosperity I said, I shall never be removed," . . .
but God hid his face, "and I was troubled."
(Ps. 30:6f.)

But then when he gets to the Lord right humbly and sees his proper relation to him, man finds that he is not a mere beast. Modern theological writing is so full of this theme of his duality, his misery, and his dignity that we need not labor the point, but it is helpful to recall the rest of the psalmist's picture of him:

"Thou hast made him a little less than divine
and hast crowned him with dignity and majesty,
Thou dost make him ruler over the works of thy hands,
all things thou hast put under his feet." (*Ps. 8:5f.*)

In God's name the psalmist says:

"Because he hath set his love upon me, therefore will
I deliver him,
I will set him on high, because he hath known my name,"
(*Ps. 91:14*)

and in his own name,

"The Lord will perfect that which concerneth me:
Thy mercy, O Lord, endureth forever:
Forsake not the works of thine own hands."
(*Ps. 138:8 KJV*)

"Into thine hand I commit my spirit:
Thou has redeemed me, faithful God." (*Ps. 31:5*)

Is there any other explanation of man that does equal justice to the truth about him? As the Psalms reveal man in all his impotence, so also they declare that God's "condescension has made me great." (Ps. 18:35) If this double teaching of the Psalter is not an honest facing of the reality, where shall we find it?

One of the great questions to be decided in our age is the extent to which a man is truly responsible for his actions. How to reckon fully with the forces that play upon man which are not under his control and, at the same time, to do justice to the fullest responsibility of which he is capable are among the most baffling contemporary problems. The clock is not to be turned back to the day when medical and other sciences had not yet studied the diseases of man as they affect antisocial behavior. But to forget man's answerability to God, to forget that which differentiates him from a rat, is to rob him of his true nature.

One of the most moving passages in modern literature, one which wrestles with the problem of man's identity and arrives where the Psalms arrive, one which lays hold upon us because of its truth, is the poem, written by Dietrich Bonhoeffer in prison shortly before his martyr's death and translated into English under the title, "Who Am I?" In the first part he tells of the favorable impression he made on his fellow prisoners and guards, that of "one accustomed to win"; in the second of what a miserable creature he is to himself:

> Weary and empty at praying, at thinking, at making,
> Faint and ready to say farewell to it all.

Then he asks:

Who am I? This or the other?
Am I one person today and tomorrow another?
  Am I both at once? A hypocrite before others,
  And before myself a contemptible, woebegone weakling?
Or is something within me still like a beaten army
Fleeing in disorder from victory already achieved?
  Who am I? They mock me, these lonely questions of
    mine.
  Whoever I am, Thou knowest, O God, I am Thine! [1]

"The business of the preacher," it has often been said, "is to tell people who they are." In a time when the depravity of man is so emphasized, we recall that the generation that produced a Hitler produced also in 1945 this word from Karl Jaspers:

Thousands in Germany have sought, or at least have found, death in opposition to the Government. We who survive have not sought death. We could have sought death in the war; when the lawlessness of the regime showed itself openly on the 30th June, 1934; or in the robbery, deportation, and murder of our Jewish friends and fellow-citizens; and when in 1938 throughout the whole of Germany the synagogues—the houses of God—were, to our indelible shame and guilt, burnt to the ground. When our Jewish friends were taken away, we did not go out into the streets and cry aloud until we also met our death. We preferred to remain in life, for the weak, even if justifiable reason, that our death would not in any way have helped. It is our fault that we are still alive. It demands that we should take on us the consequences of being alive in such conditions.[2]

What is man? Who are we? Who in prosperous America is ready to assume "the consequences of being alive" in the conditions of our day?

The Individual and Society

A second question, similar to the first, also demands our utterly honest searching if we are to live aright or even survive in our generation: What is the proper relation between man and his fellow? We referred in the preceding section to man's loneliness among a race of "outsiders." "You were at that time separated from Christ, alienated from the commonwealth of Israel, and strangers to the covenants of promise, having no hope and without God in the world." (Eph. 2:12) A man who stands outside of the people of God and cannot recollect the covenants runs the risk of losing both hope and God. Is not this loneliness, which is the sad lot of the people without God, one reason for the mass mind, conformity to the crowd, and loss of independence that characterize our time? Having no standard of reference outside self, the lonely self seeks security in a false subpersonal relationship which takes the form of imitation and seeks to avoid being thought queer. The thousands of these lonely selves become like marbles rubbing against each other in a big box rather than members of the Body of Christ, in which each part fulfills its function in the life of the whole.

Because the Psalms are often thought of as the classic expression of personal religion, it is sometimes forgotten that they are also the hymns of the Jewish community and the proven instruments of corporate faith. When the psalmists cry "out of the depths," they escape from those depths by identifying themselves with the hope of Israel. They find their problems too hard for them until they come into the sanctuary of God (Ps. 73:17) or join the multitude making a pilgrimage to his house "in the voice of praise and thanksgiving, among such as keep holy-day" (Ps. 42:4f. BCP).

Some sixty-five of the Psalms refer to the Temple. How easy it is to miss the reference in many of these passages! "I will dwell in the house of the Lord forever." (Ps. 23:6) "Come in, enter," says the Hebrew, "let us worship and bow down." (Ps. 95:6) "Thy way, O God, is in the sanctuary." (Ps. 77:13) "Who shall ascend into the hill of the Lord, or who shall stand in his holy place?" (Ps. 24:3) It is undoubtedly difficult for us today to read the pronouns "I" or "me" or "my" in the same corporate sense that Israel used them to refer to itself, the nation. "Many a time have they afflicted me [Israel] from my youth" (Ps. 129:1); "thou art my trust from my youth . . . I am as a wonder unto many; but thou art my strong refuge." (Ps. 71:5, 7) When the Psalmist says, "I will remember the years of the right hand of the Most High," he is recalling God's redemption of the whole people who were "sons of Jacob and

Joseph." (Ps. 77:10, 15 BCP) Often these allusions to the nation's history, or to its focal point, the Temple on Mt. Zion, are not easily identifiable.

But at other times the reference to corporate worship is direct and evident. "I was glad when they said unto me, Let us go into the house of the Lord." (Ps. 122:1) "How amiable are thy tabernacles, O Lord of hosts! My soul longeth, yea even fainteth for the courts of the Lord." "Blessed are they that dwell in thy house . . . A day in thy courts is better than a thousand." (Ps. 84:1, 2, 4, 10)

> "My soul thirsteth for God, for the living God,
> When shall I come and appear before God?"

or more probably, "when shall I come to see the face of God?" in the sense of attendance at the sanctuary.

> "Send out thy light and thy truth [thy favor and thy faithful dealing],
> Let them lead me,
> Let them bring me unto thy holy hill,
> and to thy tabernacles." (*Pss. 42:2; 43:3*)

> "One thing have I desired of the Lord,
> that will I seek after . . .
> to behold the beauty of the Lord,
> and to inquire in his temple." (*Ps. 27:4*)

> "Enter into his gates with thanksgiving
> and into his courts with praise." (*Ps. 100:4*)

Our concern at this point is to determine whether what the psalmists are saying about interpersonal relationships is true or not. They find fellowship in a worshipping community. They consider it highly important to gather to hear the record of God's action read and the "covenants of promise" recalled. They "inquire" or think together in the Temple and, in thinking, thank God. They find here the healing forces of forgiveness, understanding and sympathy, which, as in a family, determine in large measure the health of those who "are no more strangers and foreigners, but fellow citizens with the saints, and of the household of God" (Eph. 2:19).

Contrast with this the remark of the German factory girl quoted at a conference in Bossey, who said, "Friendship? I don't go in for that anymore. I would rather not be disappointed." One of the Asians at the conference thereupon exclaimed, "Thank God that we still live in religious cultures even though they are non-Christian." But just as secularism is divisive, so also non-Christian cultures are divisive, and the world everywhere is so full of centrifugal forces that it threatens to fly apart.

The tragedy is that the Church also is guilty of forgetting the communion of saints. If it stresses adherence to creeds or payment of tithes, or the performance of sacraments, or attendance at sermons, or obedience to rules, or even the study of the gospel, all of which are important, but neglects the gathering of God's people in Christian fellowship, it is no longer the true Church.

People have lost—or never found—interest in the needs of others, [*wrote the late Bishop of Oxford in his first book,*] and they have treated their fellows as curious spectacles, to be gossiped and wondered about, but not as living souls to be helped, strengthened and developed. [*He questions whether a young man or woman at confirmation is told first about a society of people or told*] that he must believe the creeds, know the catechism, keep the commandments, and be regular at early services.[3]

He shows how the teaching of the Church is best communicated from friend to friend, and how the search for the Lord himself is the bond which unites and makes all people interesting. In the present decade (even more than forty years ago) it is essential for "brothers to dwell together in unity" (Ps. 133:1), and to find that unity in serving the Lord through helping each other.

For as the Lord builds up Jerusalem, he is always gathering together the outcasts of Israel, including people like the poor factory-girl for whom friendship was passé. In the fellowship "he heals the broken in heart and binds up their wounds." (Ps. 147:2, 3) And in this relationship the individual achieves freedom, for the artificial, nonpersonal imitation of neighbors gives way to a triangular relationship between a man, his neighbor, and God, which is the only guarantee of both an ordered society and liberty for every member of it.

The Meaning of History

Having examined the truth of the psalmists' statements about the nature of man and his relation to his fellow, we turn now to the psalmists' view of history. This view is reflected when they undertake to answer the questions: What is man's destiny? Has history any meaning?

Before we study the psalmists' views, let us first observe some contemporary pictures of the ends of time. A generation or two ago a French astronomer, Camille Flammarion, drew a striking picture of the end of the world, in which he saw the last tribes of earth expiring of cold and hunger as the shroud of eternal ice closed over, not only the long-defunct northern centers of civilization, but the torrid zones also.

A modern counterpart to that imagery is E. B. White's description of "The Morning of the Day They Did It." [4] Two army officers in space lose the pull of gravity, the pull of conscience, the pull of duty, and even the "pull of dames." In other words responsibility and love are both dead. A few sentences from this essay reflect the views of the imaginary author who escapes to "an inferior planet, at a very great distance from the sun." The earth has been destroyed because these officers, who had ceased to care, released

> myriads of bright points of destruction where the Weapon was arriving, each pyre in the characteristic shape of an artichoke.

There is, of course, a mild irony in the fact that it was the United States that was responsible. Insofar as it can be said of any country that it had human attributes, the United States was well-meaning . . . it's just that in any matter involving love, or high explosives, one can never foresee all the factors.

Those last days! There were so many religions in conflict, each ready to save the world with its own dogma, each perfectly intolerant of the other. . . . It was a time of debauch and conversion. . . . Children early formed the habit of gaining all their images at second hand, by looking at a screen; they grew up believing that anything perceived directly was vaguely fraudulent. . . . There was really never a moment when a child, or even a man, felt free to look away from the television screen—for fear he might miss the one clue that would explain everything.[5]

If there still are men capable of painting a picture of the end of time a century hence, what will that picture be? And what will actually happen in the end? Ashes or ice? Or supposing that life as we know it can be sustained on another planet—a long leap—will mankind now on earth transfer his abode to it and then find no more meaning in its existence there? Does the earthly human race, like an individual, spend its years like "a vain show" (Ps. 39:6) to be cut off without trace, without significance, without anyone's knowledge it has ever been?

We live by pictures, we grow toward the likeness of the pictures that dominate our minds. But even those pictures which convey the most truth are not wholly adequate. We have not guaranteed the accuracy of the psalmists' historical or scientific statements. We insist rather that we pierce the passing thought forms to discover what the authors of this literature are fundamentally concerned to express. There is a great plan of God, they assert by way of answer, which is being worked out in the affairs of man. Even more important than that assertion is the assumption, shining through these poems at so many points, that God in his love for his children can do without the changes and chances of the world, but that neither the world nor man can do without God.

Three of the longer psalms, 78, 105, and 106, review God's work in Israel's history. They assert that it was God's action that brought his people into their new land, and sustained them there. "Give ear, my people, to my law"—i.e., consider how God educated each generation, his people in Egypt, again at the time of the Judges, again in the rejection of Eli's family and the choice of David, "that they might set their hope in God, and not forget the works of God, but keep his commandments" (Ps. 78:7). In 105 God is faithful to the covenant he made with Israel "that they might keep his statutes and observe his laws" (Ps. 105:45). The lesson of 106, which describes realistically Israel's disobedience, is that God is ever ready to receive his people's penitence and to give them a fresh start.

God does not work in vain. From the Exodus, "Judah was his sanctuary and Israel his dominion" (Ps. 114:2). The mountains did not skip, nor the water of Jordan turn back, nor the flint become a spring by coincidence. This nation was set apart for a sacred purpose—to be a people in whom God's will should be done.

Never fully seen, always beyond man's comprehension, God was revealing his purpose and leading his people to it.

"He spoke unto them in the cloudy pillar;
they kept his testimonies and the ordinance
that he gave them." (*Ps. 99:7*)
"The way is in the sea, and thy path in the great waters,
and thy footsteps are not known.
Thou leddest thy people like a flock
by the hand of Moses and Aaron." (*Ps. 77:19f.*)

Thus, despite all man's opposition, God is working his purpose out.

And how sad it is when his people resist his design! In all this literature there is scarcely a psalm more filled with pathos than the 81st, with its promise, its disobedience, and its lament:

"Hear, O my people, while I admonish you,
O Israel, if you would but listen to me! . . .
I am the Lord thy God, who brought you out of the land
of Egypt.
Open your mouth wide, and I will fill it.
But my people did not listen to my voice
and Israel would have none of me . . .
O that my people would listen to me,
that Israel would walk in my ways! . . .

I would feed you with the finest of the wheat,
  and with honey from the rock I would satisfy you."
(*Ps. 81:8,10,11,13,16*)

In a time of abundance that fancies itself to be also realistic, there may be little appreciation of such prophetic idealism as the following:

All the ends of the world shall remember and turn unto the Lord;
  and all the kindreds of the nations shall worship before thee.
For the kingdom is the Lord's, and he is the governor among the nations." (*Ps. 22:27f.*)

The point is that God's purpose moves history toward an appointed goal; man does not need to wander aimlessly on earth, or, as we shall see, even in space. We come back to our original question about the truth of the Psalms and ask: Does the interpretation of history which pictures man only on his way to ashes make more sense, prove more consistent, lay hold upon more of man's capacities, and give him better guidance for life than these Psalms?

God in Nature

For a few moments we turn our consideration to the psalmists' assertions about the place in God's plan of the natural world in order to test these assertions for their fundamental accord with reality.

> "The earth is the Lord's, and the fulness thereof
> [everything in it]
> the world, and they that dwell therein.
> For he hath founded it upon the seas
> and established it upon the floods." (*Ps. 24:1f.*)

A changing cosmology has not altered that fundamental truth.

> "The heavens declare the glory of God,
> and the firmament showeth his handiwork.
> Day unto day uttereth speech
> and night unto night showeth knowledge."
> (*Ps. 19:1f*)

That is, the testimony of the natural world to God is unbroken, for the order of creation is grounded in the mind of the Creator,

> "Who layeth the beams of his chambers in the waters.
> Who maketh the clouds his chariot, who walketh upon
> the wings of the wind." (*Ps. 104:3*)

Still today the winds are his agents and fire his servants, not by caprice but by a well-ordered Providence.

> "Thou makest the outgoings of the morning and
> evening to rejoice." (*Ps. 65:8*)

"Thou crownest the year with thy goodness and
thy paths drop fatness." (*Ps. 65:11*)

Are the beauties of dawn and sunset accidental, or do they correspond to a purpose in the ground of all being? Is there no plan grounded in mind behind the yearly harvest? As we remember again the danger of annihilation, either we despair or hope depending on our acceptance of these words:

"Of old hast thou laid the foundation of the earth:
and the heavens are the work of thy hands.
They shall perish, but thou shalt endure:
yea, all of them shall wax old like a garment;
As a vesture shalt thou change them,
and they shall be changed,
But thou are art the same,
and thy years have no end.
The children of thy servants shall continue,
and their seed shall be established before thee.
(*Ps. 102:25-28*)

By which picture shall we live? Where shall we find the truth?

God the Source of Man's Hope

Finally, we examine the most important question of all: Do the Psalms offer us an accurate picture of God in whom we may place our hope? If they do, then not to love and serve him is the lie which above all other lies must be eradicated. If they do not, in what are they wrong?

It is true that some of the Psalms appeal to God to act for his self-interest on the ground that if the worshipper is killed God will have so much the less praise. It is true that God is spoken of as napping, negligent, needing to be prodded. And as he is the God of a persecuted people who are highly conscious of their national destiny, it is not surprising that he is thought about sometimes in nationalistic terms. Other writings, in the Old Testament as well as the New, correct the view of some of the Psalms that his rewards and punishments, of a material kind, are in direct proportion to the virtue or vice of men. Expressions such as "the Lord shall have them in derision" need to be studied with care. For the Christian, the picture of God given here will always be tested by its correspondence with the face of Jesus Christ.

And it is worth making such a test. Remembering what we have already seen of God's rule over history and nature, we explore one of the great psalms, 103, for its teaching about God's character, his love for his people, his forgiveness, his Fatherhood, his renewing power, his rightness and his patience, his outreaching goodness, and his strength in the midst of human frailty.

> "Bless the Lord, my whole being,
> and all within me his holy name."

The name is the key that unlocks the memory of his character as revealed in his deeds, and it is holy, separate, to be revered, far above every other name. Does a Christian find the acts of God, as seen by this poet, consonant with the deeds of Jesus?

> Bless the Lord, my whole being,
>   and forget none of his benefits,
> Who forgives all your iniquities,
>   who heals all your sicknesses,
> Who redeems your life from the Pit,
>   who crowns you with devotion and compassion;
> Who satisfies your desire with good,
>   that you may renew your youth like the eagle.

These are some of God's benefits to the individual: his forgiveness and healing (the two go together), his preservation of life and renewal of strength, and especially his acts of loyal devotion or affectionate loyalty (commonly translated *mercy* or *loving kindness*) mentioned four times in these few lines. These are the deeds which reveal God's character.

But he is not a private God for a prosperous individual or even a prosperous nation. In history he has customarily performed acts by which the oppressed have been vindicated and delivered. These acts reveal his justice, his action on the part of right, which he made known to Moses and to all successive generations. The chief characteristic again is his forgiving, steadfast love:

The Lord is merciful and gracious
slow to anger and abounding in devotion.
Not always does he chide,
and not forever does he frown. . . .
As the heavens form a canopy over the earth,
his devotion is high over his worshippers,
As far as the east is from the west,
so far has he removed our transgressions from us;
As a father pitieth his children
so the Lord pities his worshippers.
For he knows our frame,
he remembers that we are dust.[6]

By such lines the way is prepared for the Gospel teaching that the heavenly Father is merciful. Here is the Old Testament background for the story of the Prodigal Son.

God's devotion is not only for past ages but also for the present; it extends even to children's children, to those who keep his covenant, for

"he has prepared his throne in the heavens,
and his kingdom rules over all."

And this is why even the angels or messengers of God who do his business, all his armies and all his servants, all his works in all places of his dominion, are bidden to praise him. The life to which our Lord summons us is also the life of his kingdom.[7]

Although this picture of God is only a fragment of the

whole, which should include, besides his grace, his holiness, his justice, and the severity of his demand, what the Psalms teach us of his care is enough to humble us and then "quicken us again." They give a consistent picture of an almighty Creator who also reaches out to each of his children with infinite love.

But the issue is truth. In what the Psalms have told us about man, the community, history, nature, and God himself, are they right? We walk by faith, not by sight. The truth we have been examining is not one to be demonstrated in the same way as is a proposition in geometry. But if these declarations of this ancient hymn book, for all their difficulties and imperfections, nevertheless make more sense of these vital matters than any rival theories, if they present a picture of reality that is consistent, if they invite us to lay hold on life to the full, if they offer the richest gifts that the Author of life bestows, and at the same time summon and strengthen us to respond to its greatest demands, then even this discussion partakes of an urgency similar to that of Richard Baxter's sermons, which he called the words of a "dying man to dying men."

By what or by whom do we live? In honesty we cannot evade the question. If we profess to live by the psalmists' God and in practice fall into contemporary forms of idolatry, we are hypocrites. But if the Lord is our God, then to be in correspondence with reality we must grow in the knowledge and love of him, for he is a living God and his spirit never allows us to remain static. Again, if the Psalms are true, as we approach God we need such a garment of praise as they provide when we should otherwise feel naked.

Truth is the issue. It will never rest until it prevails in our homes, in our schools, in our professions and business, in our governments, and in our world. The indicative thus becomes an imperative, bidding us in the psalmists' words to "ride forth victoriously for the cause of truth and to defend the right," (Ps. 45:4) humble and modest, but never resting until God's "way is known upon earth, his saving health among all nations." [8]

III.

THE NATURE AND SOLUTION OF THE PSALMISTS' TROUBLES

In testing the permanence of the psalmists' experiences and the truth of their fundamental assumptions, it was apparent that although their outbursts are sometimes violent, harsh, and hateful, they compare well as poets with the authors of much pious verse because they are honest. They are not awkward in God's presence. If they sometimes protest against their lot, they are also spontaneous, wholehearted, and therefore express the feelings and the minds of successive ages in a way that the sentimental can never do.

To participate as far as possible in the psalmists' honest struggle is our purpose in this chapter. Earlier we discussed the problem of the vast difference between the conditions of the psalmists' life and our own as we tried to face frankly the fact that much of what they said of old does not fit our tongues. But also it was clear that there are basic human problems that remain fairly constant: apostasy (which may be interpreted as man's abandonment of the self which God wills, for a self which man chooses), pride, doubt, the burden of a sinful past, injustice, and alienation. No affluent society has eliminated these. It may even have increased them.

We mentioned earlier that our attitude toward the Psalms had changed even in the last decade. How? Today we penetrate more deeply into their striving in order to share it. This does not mean that the study of textual problems has become unimportant, nor that questions of translation and poetic form can be overlooked. It does not mean that the use of the Psalms made through the years in Christian theology or Jewish piety is outmoded. There are delights for the scholar, as we shall see in the next chapter, along many avenues of Psalm study. Meticulous attention to detail inevitably undergirds proper conclusions, and the dangers of hasty generalization are well known. But the prolegomena must not occupy us to the point where we fail to come to the heart of the matter. All around us are people hungry for light on such problems as those with which the psalmists deal. Even in the churches millions only half-hear what the Psalms say. Can we help these people to share in the battle and then in the victory?

The Struggle with Apostasy

To illustrate a few of the difficulties that beset the interpreter of a psalm, we may refer briefly to a poem which appears twice in the Psalter, as 14 and as 53. Although these are variant forms of the same psalm, both have been corrupted and neither represents what the author wrote. It is necessary, first, to establish a text. We try to do so by putting the two together, supplying a missing half line from one, following the Greek that makes good sense against the Hebrew that doesn't, using the poetic structure and the studies of the scholars for such help as they can give, until there emerge twelve lines of intelligible Hebrew. Then comes the problem of how to express this text in English. For example, which is best:

> The fool says in his heart. (RSV)
> Fools said in their heart.
> The foolish man says to himself.
> A fool said in his heart.
> The fools thought in their heart.

Heart might more accurately be rendered *mind, said* means also *thought, fool* is collective, the tense may be either present or past. We must make a decision even for an inadequate translation in order to proceed.

Fools say to themselves,
  "There is no God."
They deal corruptly, abominably,
  nobody doing right.
The Lord looks down from heaven
  on the human race

To see whether any act wisely
  in seeking after God.
All have strayed, altogether are vile,
  nobody doing right,
[nobody acting wisely in seeking for God]
  not a single one.
Have they no knowledge whatsoever,
  all the evil doers,
Who devour my people as they eat bread,
  and do not call on the Lord?
There they are in consternation
  where no dread once was,
for the Lord scatters the bones of the godless,
  who are foiled because he rejects them.
Would that from Zion might come forth
  the rescue of Israel!
As the Lord restores his people's fortunes,
  let Jacob rejoice, let Israel be glad.

But then, even when the text is established and the translation decided upon, how are the words to be interpreted? Does "there is no God" mean that the fools are atheists, or that in effect they are saying that God is inoperative: "God is not concerned here"? Does the term *fool* imply intellectual aberration or moral perversity also? Does the phrase *my people* mean the Lord's people or the poet's people; who speaks, and who are the oppressors—priests who eat the Lord's bread without worshipping him or foreign tyrants? There is the further question as to whether St. Paul was right in finding in these verses a reference to universal sin.[1] Truly there are no short cuts to proper understanding of his poem.

But what is even more important than the correct text, the best translation, the most probable interpretation, and the use of the psalm in the New Testament is whether its truth can come alive in our hearts. Does this truth find us? Do we see here a connection between mental and moral folly, between apostasy and dread, between theology and conduct, between religion and ethics? Although we may hesitate to say of others:

> All have strayed, altogether are vile,
> Nobody doing right,

is it not certain that each of us, measuring ourselves by each other, forgetting God, has a long record of corrupt and abominable dealing, only part of which we consciously realize? Is it not true for us that this lack of allegiance to God (since allegiance forms part of the Hebrew concept of the knowledge of God) is the source of our injustice to our fellow man—even church people sometimes "devour"—and later the cause of our consternation? Does God not bring frustration along this road? Should we not also pray God to rescue or restore his people? When we seek him faithfully, shall we not become less of a problem to our fellows and to ourselves, and more capable of right action, wisdom, confidence, and rejoicing?

Pride

In Psalm 14/53 the poet struggles with the apostasy of the human race and with its unhappy consequences. However much he may convict us of our sin, there is no clear sense of personal guilt in the psalm itself. In another psalm the author grapples with the pride at the core of his own being. That pride, which is both national and ecclesiastical, is very similar to the patriotic self-righteousness often attributed to American churchmen.

Psalm 30 speaks to an affluent society which is seeking for security, but not really finding it. The psalmist's method is, first to tell of his rescue and the character of God that saved him, then to reveal the nature of his trouble and his wrestling with it, and finally to return to joy and praise that deliverance has come. How artistic is his arrangement: a major key, a minor key, a major key; thesis, antithesis, synthesis; praise at the beginning for God's character, realization next that even religious men make idols or substitutes for God and need forgiveness and help, finally praise for God's action in response to man's cry!

The psalmist begins:

> I extol thee, Lord, for thou hast drawn me up
> and not let my enemies rejoice over me.

The picture suggested by the verb *drawn up* is that of a bucket being pulled up from the bottom of a well.

O Lord my God,
I cried to thee and thou didst hear me.
Lord, thou didst bring me up from hell,
reviving me at the point of descent to the Pit.

The figure of the first verse is sustained. The author, or his nation, or both were almost at the point of extinction, almost at the bottom of the abyss.

Sing praises to the Lord, you his saints,
and give thanks to his holy name!

For his name is the key to the remembrance of his acts and of his character:

Though his anger is fleeting, his favor is life long,
in the evening lodges weeping, but by morning joy!

These first five verses are beautiful and significant in themselves, but note the five verses which follow, the part of the poem which particularly speaks to our condition, where the psalmist exposes his false pride, the insecurity to which it led, and his struggle to find firm footing once more.

But I said in my security
"I shall never be shaken, Lord.
In thy favor thou hast made my mountain stand firm."
Thou didst hide thy face; I was put to confusion.

The mountain is the hill on which stands the Temple, the focal point of Israel's political and ecclesiastical life. God has blessed the nation; God has favored its religion.

How contemporary this all sounds! With our indestructible power who shall harm us? Here we are secure—only to find that this confident pride is not our strength, but our weakness.

"This is the tragedy of America, that lacking a sense of spiritual involvement in world tragedy, she invites eventual cataclysm on America and finds herself with no faculty to apprehend its meaning and potential." "There is no fundamental sense of present judgment, no deep sense of identity with and responsibility for what has happened . . . no urgent conviction that reform is necessary," [2] and no realization that renewal is a gift of God's grace.

I said in my security,
  "I shall never be shaken, Lord.
In thy favor thou hast made my mountain stand firm."

Not only our nation, but the Church also, despite many warnings, rests secure in its temple on its holy mountain, which it forgets stands also under God's judgment.

"She cannot keep women in a place which denies that they are participating in the maturing of humanity. She cannot do her pastoral work in ways which assume that psychology is a form of unbelief. She cannot express her theology without reference to the philosophies which express the confidence and also the critical modesty of our scientific culture." [3]

Yet what the Church cannot do with impunity she keeps

on doing. She persists in the notion that her mountain stands firm, and sometimes silences those who call attention to the shaking. Can the psalm bring her to her true self?

I kept calling to thee, Lord,
and made supplication to my God:[4]
"What profit in my blood if I sink to the Pit?
Does dust give thee thanks or declare thy faithfulness?"

Although our view of the hereafter has changed, let not that fact obscure for us the summons of these lines, to begin where our Lord began, with a sense of God's saving love and the nearness of judgment, and then to "get to the Lord right humbly" in penitence for the way we have trusted in our mountains—words, or armaments, or church memberships—or for the way in which we have ignored the tragedy of the world and the complacency of the Church.

"Hear, Lord, and take pity on me,
Lord, be thou my helper."

The bucket had plunged almost to the bottom of the well; the strong mountain was really weak although it was the site of God's house. God had been forced to hide his face from the proud; but because love rather than anger is his dominant characteristic, when we humble ourselves and seek his forgiveness, trusting in him rather than any *thing*, the night of weeping becomes the morn of song.

Thou hast turned my wailing into dancing,
thou hast put off my sackcloth and robed me with gladness.
Let my heart sing thy praise without ceasing,
Lord, my God, let me thank thee forever.

Wrestling with Despair

We turn now to another picture of struggle for faith. Precisely what has plunged the author of Psalm 130 into the depths we are not told; but the eight short lines show its author climbing out. He is humble, willing to wait, and confident of Israel's future in which his personal security lies. The national reference of the psalm is clear even while through it an individual expresses his own plight.

Out of the depths I call to thee, Lord!
hear my voice.
Let thy ears be attentive
to the voice of my supplications.

As soon as the suppliant has called God, his battle against despair is on the way to victory. The decisive first step in the struggle is to know the source of help. When man truly waits upon God, every good can follow. When the fundamental orientation of life is wrong, all is wrong.

If thou shouldest store up iniquities, Lord,
who could stand?

But with thee is forgiveness
  that thou mayest be revered.

As in Psalm 14, so here also is the recognition that all men are caught in the human predicament of sin. No man can stand or endure if God should keep account of his "iniquities"—a conveniently ambiguous word which means both the sin and its consequences, or punishment. If God were to pay man his just due, there would be no hope; but because God makes moral distinctions even between sinner and sinner, he forgives. If he did not, there could be only moral chaos and no proper reverence for him.

I wait for the Lord,
  my whole being waits for his word.

The word of command is also the word of promise.

My whole being hopes for the Lord
  more than watchmen for the morning.
For with the Lord there is devotion
  and with him is plentiful redemption,
and it is he who will redeem Israel
  from all his iniquities.

The forgiving Lord is also the source of all affectionate loyalty, out of which springs redemption, which in turn includes rescue from the depths of sin. To trust in the Lord, to wait for him, to hope in him, is the way of deliverance. "I am sunk," says modern man even in a time of plenty, and, like this psalmist, he is not explicit as to the cause. To him the psalmist replies, "Begin with a forgiving God; and for the rest, wait."

The Weight of Sin

Psalm 130 is a beautiful expression of patient faith, but to understand the profundity of the psalmist's struggle with the weight of his own sin we must examine what has rightly been called "perhaps the noblest penitential hymn in all the world," Psalm 51. The source of this author's major trouble, as he rightly sees, is the evil he has done. From the time of his birth he has been entangled in a world-complex of error and wrong; he would have no difficulty in repeating the words of the general confession, "There is no health in us."

His problem is the restoration of broken relationships, not alone with his neighbors but ultimately with God. No superficial patching will suffice so long as that primary relationship is wrong. But God is more eager to heal the breach than man is, although he will never force his love. As man waits for God, so God waits for him—for his repentance, his recognition of the true situation, his sorrow for all the past, and his definite turning away from it to a new way of life characterized by a new spirit.

> Take pity on me, Lord, according to thy devotion,
> in the abundance of thy mercies blot out my transgressions.

The initiative in the healing process is the Lord's love, for he alone is the source of forgiveness and the cleansing which is possible when man knows or recognizes or confesses his true condition. Even an individual or, if he speaks collectively, a nation which may be innocent in respect to others is never clean before God.

Wash me thoroughly from my iniquity
  and cleanse me from my sin.
For I know my transgressions
  and my sin is before me continually.
Against thee, thee only, have I sinned,
  and done what is evil in thy sight,
but thou art righteous when thou dost give sentence
  and blameless when thou dost judge.
In iniquity I was born
  and in sin my mother engendered me.

This is not to say that the act of procreation is sinful, but that man is born into a world in which iniquity is endemic. The Lord is stronger, however, than even the vast complex of man's sin; the only condition of restoration is that hearts be open:

Thou dost delight in faithfulness in secret,
  and in a hidden place thou dost teach me wisdom.
Thou dost purge me with hyssop that I may be clean,
  thou dost wash me that I may be whiter than snow.

Thou dost make me hear joy and gladness,
the bones which thou hast crushed rejoice.
Hide thy face from my sins
and blot out all my iniquities.
Create for me a pure heart, Lord,
and renew a firm spirit within me.
Do not cast me from thy presence
nor take thy holy spirit from me.
Restore to me the joy of thy help
and may a willing spirit unhold me,
That I may teach transgressors thy ways
and sinners may return to thee.
Deliver me from violence,
Lord God who dost save me;
My tongue will shout thy virtue,
and my mouth declare thy praise.
For thou dost not delight in sacrifice
and if I give a burnt offering thou art not pleased.
The sacrifices due the Lord are a broken spirit,
a broken and a contrite heart.

Our subject—lest we forget—is the nature and solution of the psalmists' troubles. Nowhere in the Bible within so few lines is sin more graphically described, or the nature of the new spirit that follows repentance, or the results of the gift of forgiveness. At every point the psalmist speaks to us of the twentieth century and of our plight with relevance never exceeded in more than two thousand years.

In his description of sin and its power—the tyranny of a misused past, the psalmist anticipates modern psychology. Sin defiles man, and makes him need a thorough washing. It plagues his imagination, for it is so continually before him that he cannot seem to escape it. It troubles his mind and upsets his spirit. It robs him of happiness. It grinds his bones. Because of it he feels alienated from God, who alone can restore the broken relationship and heal the broken heart. How contemporary this sounds! Without my wishing it, even in this prosperous society I have been caught in a great net of wrongdoing to which I too have contributed; and because of it I feel dirty, tormented in spirit, anxious, unsteady, sad and crushed. "Miserable man that I am, who will release me from this body of death?" (Rom. 7:24)

But the psalmist knows what to do, to whom to turn for the solution of his ills. Animal sacrifices or their monetary counterparts are of no avail, but with recognition of his true situation—"I know my transgressions"—the man made "lowly wise" turns to the Lord who forgives and restores. If forgiveness is one of the most important Christian teachings, here is one of the most significant pre-Christian statements of what forgiveness does. It creates a new spirit so that the forgiven sinner can begin anew his life on a different basis.

Four times the term *spirit* is used in this psalm. In verse

10 (BCP) the accompanying adjective translated *right* really means *firm* or *confident* or *stable.* In the next verse it is *pure,* separate from what is profane, or *holy.* In the next it is *willing* or *free* or *voluntary.* Five lines later the troubled spirit is literally a *broken* spirit, parallel to a contrite heart. The character of the man who repents and is remade is, therefore, confident, transparent or pure, free, and humble.

To sum up briefly the profundity of this great hymn about the mystery of God's forgiving power, the solution to man's basic trouble: (a) The psalmist looks beyond the sinner as he now is to what he may become when his mind and heart are filled with God. Life takes on another dimension. "If any one is in Christ, he is a new creation." (b) When the bones must be crushed by punishment, sorrow is inevitable; when man is contrite or crushes himself, "there is joy before the angels of God over one sinner who repents." (c) As in the vision of Isaiah in the Temple, the vision of reality leads to penitence and confession, confession to forgiveness, and forgiveness to a new sense of responsibility for others, "that I may teach transgressors thy ways, and sinners may return to thee." (d) Finally, this way of penitence and God's restoration is the way of liberty. However much we have sinned, God still desires us. Granting us the joy of his help, he calls us and uses us for his purposes. With a willing spirit he upholds us, for his service is perfect freedom. New life, new joy, new work, new freedom—these he would give us.

What to Make of Suffering

In the four psalms we have just examined, the psalmist has struggled with apostasy, pride, doubt, and the burden of past sins. But there is another baffling problem to which we must give attention, the apparent injustice of suffering.

Psalm 73 begins with what is ultimately the poet's conclusion:

> Yes, God is good to the upright,
> the Lord to the pure in heart,

but he confesses that he almost abandoned his belief in God when he confronted honestly the world's riddle: why do wicked men prosper while the good suffer?—a riddle more perplexing than ever in days of great abundance when some flourish while millions of others starve, a riddle even if it is not ordinarily given to the well-fed to recognize the true situation. The psalmist is tempted to be envious of those "successful" people who even scoff and defy God.

> But as for me, my feet almost strayed,
> my steps nearly slipped,
> for I was envious of the boastful
> when I saw the prosperity of the wicked.
> For they experience no pangs,
> whole and fat are their paunches,
> in human trouble they have no share,
> nor are they plagued with the rest of mankind.

Six verses of further description follow,

> And they say, "How can God know
> and is there knowledge with the Most High?
> Lo, these are the wicked,
> always secure, they increase in wealth.

As if the worldly good fortune of evil men were not enough, the upright man's affliction accentuates the injustice still further and tempts him to abandon his faith.

> All in vain have I kept my mind clean
> and washed in innocence my hands,
> and been plagued every day
> and chastened every morning.

But at this point he checks himself when he remembers the people who, he knows in his heart, have life's secret, the people of truth and of goodness with whom he is unwilling to break faith.

> But if I had said, "Let me speak in this way,"
> I would have been a traitor to the generation of thy children.

And therefore he goes into the sanctuary and sees what a stupid beast he has been.

> But when I thought how to understand this
> it seemed to me perplexing.

I was a brute with no understanding
  I became a beast toward thee,
Until I entered the sanctuary of God
  when I perceived their end.

There he comes to two conclusions: one of which is right, the other wrong. He is wrong in his dogmatic assertion that the wicked are like a bad dream that will soon be finished, for wickedness is not that ephemeral.

In slippery places thou dost put them,
  and dost make them fall to ruin.
How are they devastated in a moment,
  and completely finished by calamities!
They are like a dream when one wakes;
  On awaking you despise their phantoms.

But he is right—everlastingly right because he is true to his most profound experience—when he concludes that to suffer with God is better than to be prosperous without him.

But I am always with thee,
  thou dost hold my right hand,
leading me by thy counsel,
  keeping me with thee.[5]
Whom have I in heaven but thee,
  and having thee I desire nothing on earth.
Although my body and mind fail
  the Lord is my portion forever.

In sum:

> Those who are far from thee perish,
> thou dost annihilate all who are unfaithful to thee.

Again the wrong answer to the riddle is followed by the right one:

> But for me, it is best to be near God,
> I have made the Lord my refuge.

What does this psalm say to prosperous churchmen in an age of plenty?

(1) It bids us heed words of warning about privilege, such as those recently written by M. J. M. Paton regarding the "Establishment" of the Church of England:

> The disadvantage of privilege is that the nation identifies the Church with privilege, and accordingly ignores it . . . And privilege has the usual effect of making us love the gift but not the giver: we value our 'national status,' but we seem to regard the state not with love but with a kind of timorous defiance, much as government departments tend to regard the Treasury . . . Surely our task is to convert the state to the love of Christ crucified? [6]

When a nation is rich, or when a church is privileged, when all seems well with an individual, things tend to take the place of persons in the center of affection, and we betray our Lord.

(2) Conversely, when suffering strikes with all its seem-

ing waste, reflection in the presence of God may reveal that even pain may be the way to illumination and man's highest good. On this subject we must neither write too easily nor speak glibly. Too much pain, as we recognize, has the effect of deadening character. Our Lord cured pain as if it never could be endured. But no pain at all may be even worse if it results in the refusal to share in mankind's lot. Comfort and ease may mean isolation and loneliness, a death to be feared more than the dissolution of the body. And if this problem of the injustice of suffering has never been solved, despite all the attention paid to it through the ages, still the Cross provides our best clue. In the end our Lord endured pain as if it never could be cured.

The author of the Epistle to the Hebrews goes so far as to say that Christ learned obedience though the things that he suffered. (Heb. 5:8) In suffering, as in no other way, he identified himself to the full with every suffering creature. Reaching out in a similar acceptance of suffering, God's children find God himself. St. Paul therefore says in effect, "Most gladly will I suffer that the power of Christ may rest upon me." (2 Cor. 12:9)

Not many men can repeat those words. Most of us would elect for ourselves probably, and for our loved ones almost certainly, not to suffer. There is little warrant in the Gospels for us to inflict upon ourselves unnecessary suffering. But when suffering comes, as it inevitably does to anyone at all sensitive to the woes of people all about him, can we learn from this psalmist that to be near God is our highest good? Can we find God before us in the midst of the world's ills which he has made his own? Can we firmly refuse corrupting isolation from trouble, and elect to share some part of the world's pain, finding glory in it because it brings us closer to our fellows and to God? In such a choice we shall be faithful to the generation of God's children, to this psalmist and to the Cross.

It was said to one of Sir Frances Drake's sailors, "You don't seem to have profited much by all your seafaring"; whereupon he replied, "No, but I have served the finest Captain who ever sailed the seas!" [7]

Man's Worth

This examination of the nature and solution of the psalmists' troubles would be sadly incomplete if it omitted his wrestling with the equally profound problem, the place of man, struggling to find meaning in his moral effort, amid all the wonder of the immensities of God's creation.

Eight centuries ago Ibn Ezra recognized the unique contribution of Psalm 139 when he declared, "This psalm is very glorious; in these five books there is none like it." For this psalm marks the culmination of Old Testament teaching about God, while expressing the most exalted view of the worth and dignity of man.

> Lord thou dost search me
>   and thou dost know me.
> Thou knowest when I sit and rise,

thou discoverest my thought from afar.
Thou dost test me when I journey or recline
and art acquainted with all my ways.

Literally, thou dost sift—as through a sieve—my path and my couch.

For there is not a word on my tongue
but that thou, Lord, dost know it all.
Behind and before thou dost besiege me
and lay thy hand over me.
Such knowledge is too wonderful for me,
it is so high that I cannot reach it.

But the Lord who besieges us and puts his hand over us is not our enemy, but our divine companion and our most precious friend.

Whither could I go from thy spirit
or whither flee from thy presence?
If I climb to heaven, thou are there,
or spread my bed in hell, lo thou art there!
Though I take the wings of the dawn
or dwell in the remote part of the sea,[8]
there also thy hand leads me
and thy right hand holds me.
When I say, "Darkness surely will cover me,
and the light about me will be night,"
Even darkness is not too dark for thee[9]
and night is as bright as the day.

Here the God who knows each of his creatures is recognized as present everywhere in his creation. The God of personal experience and the God of Nature are one. Amos had declared that there is no hiding even in the bottom of the sea from the divine punishment, Jonah that there is no escape from the pursuing will of the Lord who calls Israel to carry his message to those whom Israel hated most. Plato had written that no man is so small as to be able to hide by creeping into a deep hole in the earth, nor so high that he can fly away from the penalty for his deeds.[10] But here in Psalm 139 the psalmist does not flee up or down, east or west. He does not try to hide under cover of darkness, for the God who fills the three-storied universe is reaching out not to punish but to bless.

"Little know they in truth," says St. Augustine, "that thou art ever near, even to those who set themselves furthest from thee. Thou forsakest nothing that thou has made. Not any man of flesh and blood, but thou, Lord, who madest them, canst refresh and comfort them."[11]

Unfortunately the text of the following six lines is uncertain, but the purport of the section as a whole is clear. God knows man before his birth. Even in the womb a variegated pattern was being woven very wonderfully, and God had his plan for the days that were to be. Therefore the psalmist must stand in awe before the vastness of the divine design.

> How precious to me are thy thoughts, O God!
> How vast is the sum of them!

If I count them, they are more than the sand,
  When I reach the end, I am still with thee.

Our age may rediscover a sense of the mystery of life in the immensities of interstellar space and expanding horizons beyond our earliest wildest fancies. It is possible that we may even recover the sense of worship which, Coleridge says, begins as the child of wonder and becomes the father of praise. But pantheism is not enough, any more than parochialism is enough. As we grow in our knowledge of the marvels of the universe, so we would find a sense of the purpose of the God who has given us life. As bewilderment before the eternal infinite may help us to be humble, so confidence in the "most near" may make us strong.

In the concluding lines of this psalm, after a call to God not to ignore the distinction between good and evil, couched in curses which we may well omit, the author returns from the greatness of the God without to pray to the God who is also within.

Search me, God, and know my mind.
  Test me and know my disquieting thoughts,
and see if there be any hurtful way in me,
  and lead me in the way everlasting.

The Lord of interstellar space is also in the center of the moral struggle taking place in each human heart. When in the secrecy of his innermost being a man honestly asks that God may thwart the hurtful way that is in him and lead him in the way everlasting, then he is in the company of the eternal and omnipresent Creator and Lord.

The author of Psalm 139, responding to the wonder of God's greatness in the world beyond him and the aspirations that are the counterpart of the disquieting thoughts within him, does not know of the eternal life of which Jesus has the words, but he does find companionship with the Ruler of the universe, without whom the continuation of our existence would be empty, but with whom we may face any future unafraid.

IV.

POETRY IN AN AGE OF PROSE

"Great literature is the worthy expression of permanent and universal intellectual or emotional truth." [1] In the preceding chapters we have sought to establish the permanence and potential universality of the Psalmists' basic concepts and their most significant experiences. But is the form in which these are presented a sufficient vehicle for the timeless truth contained within it?

Our prosperous age, in which history has been called "bunk," has been also a time in which the language of sixteenth- and seventeenth-century England, the language of the King James Version of the Bible, has widely been forgotten; on the other hand there have been violent protests against modern translations.

"During the last hundred years," writes Jacques Barzun "nearly every intellectual force has worked, in all innocence, against language." [2] He mentions the decline not only of English, but of French and German. "The universal barbarism of language has already gone well into the grotesque." Should therefore the student of the Psalms cling tightly to the translation given in the King James Version, the language of which is no longer the speech of our day, or, if he happens to be an Episcopalian, refuse all rivals to his Prayer Book, or, even in the face of the deterioration which he laments, find a new garment for his praise? Against the argument that this century is not a time for new translations, religious necessity must be given priority over literary scruples. The Psalms are not a collector's item; they are the daily food of hungry worshippers. To the extent that existing forms are adequate they must be maintained, for they act as a cohesive link between the parts of the whole Church, but if the language of living persons changes so radically as to choke the traditional Psalms to death, then alternative forms must be devised whereby the tradition—in a different dress—may live and grow from strength to strength.

The Nature of Hebrew Poetry

To begin at a point on which little controversy is likely, surely the Psalms should be written as poetry. The Revised Standard Version rightly indicates by the arrangement of its printing that one set of time intervals is set over against a corresponding set in a regularly recurring pattern.

Who shall ascend the hill of the Lord?

is the RSV's rendering of a half-line in Hebrew which was read probably with four accents.[3] But by themselves these words are not poetry. They become so when this series of stresses is immediately followed by a similar series:

And who shall stand in his holy place?

It is altogether fitting that this correspondence be shown so far as may be possible by the rhythm of the English translation and the identification of the lines (Hebrew half-lines) on the printed page.

A different rhythm, in which two accents match two, appears later in this psalm, which is one reason among others for belief that two poems have been combined:

Lift up your heads, O gates!
and be lifted up O ancient doors!
that the glorious King may come in.

In the preceding psalm (the 23rd) as in many others, the second half-lines of the Hebrew, hence the alternate lines in English, are shorter than the rest, because in the place of a word or syllable to carry the final accent there is a pause or rest. The RSV is therefore altogether right in printing the concluding words of that psalm, "for ever," on a line of their own. It would have brought out the rhythm better if it had used an expression such as "to the end of time" or even the repetitious "as long as I live" to render the Hebrew, which literally reads "to length of days."[4] But in this Psalm it was important to cling to the familiar.

Although three or four Psalms[5] are scarcely poetry, despite some use of quotations in 1 and 79 from earlier verse, in general the rhythms are simple and not hard to discern: 4:4, 4:3, or less frequently 2:2. Where there is a radical alteration of the metrical scheme, there is often some prosy annotation to the text. "Mixed rhythms" are very unlikely, free verse for a psalmist impossible.

If to this point we have not mentioned the balance and parallelism of ideas, that is not to ignore or minimize such parallelism. But parallelism can and does exist also in prose; that which differentiates poetry is harmonized time, in the case of Hebrew achieved through accents.

With the Psalms printed as poetry, the reader is helped to feel the rhythm. If, moreover, the prosy additions to some of the poems were printed as prose, he could be kept from stumbling over many of the obscurities of this literature.

Problems of Text and Editorial Additions

That the Psalter is the end result of a long period of editorial activity is self-evident, although one of the rewards of study is to detect more and more surely the marginal notes and corrections which editors or scribes incorporated in the text and which sometimes mar our present translations. Sometimes in the process of transmission two different traditions about a given line or clause were preserved side by side.[6] Sometimes an unusual word needed to be explained.[7] Sometimes the ancient editors felt the need to embellish.[8] Sometimes a commentator betrayed his theological interest—such as his desire to insist on the Temple at Jerusalem as the sole legitimate place of worship,[9] or to denounce idolatry,[10] to insist on the coming day of judgment,[11] and in two instances at least, to indicate that there is a possibility of desirable life after death—by inserting commentary in the text.[12] Frequently these additions occur at the beginning or the end of the psalm, where there was room on the manuscript scroll.

About one fourth of the Psalms seem to have been eight-line pieces divisible into two equal halves of four lines each. However revolutionary and difficult of accomplishment, the proposal we now put forward, is that a printed edition indicate plainly this eight-line arrangement—as other similar arrangements—and print in small type any probable intrusions into the pattern.

Psalm 122 is usually regarded as a Pilgrim psalm, either a parting greeting to Jerusalem at the end of a visit or the prayer of an old man who rejoices over his former pilgrimage. The Temple, the focal point of the journey, is mentioned in the first line and the last.

> I rejoiced when they said to me,
>   "Let us go to the house of the Lord."
> Our feet have been standing
>   within your gates, Jerusalem,
> Jerusalem, built as a city
>   wherein men gather together,[13]
> whither the tribes go up,
>   the tribes of the Lord.

Into the midst of this spontaneous rejoicing some scribe has injected a prosy note; "it is an ordinance for Israel to give thanks to the name of the Lord," or, if the text be altered, "to thank the Lord there. For there (the Hebrew says "thither") sit thrones for justice, thrones for the house of David," i.e., this is the place of the Sanhedrin. Not alone on metrical grounds is this verse and a half to be regarded as an intrusion, but the break in the form is a useful bit of supporting evidence. The poem concludes:

> Pray for the peace of Jerusalem:
>   "May your dwellings be secure.
> Peace be within your ramparts,
>   security within your battlements."
> For the sake of my brethren and friends
>   let me say, "Peace be within you!"
> For the sake of the house of the Lord our God,
>   let me seek your good.

Is the poem stronger or weaker without those middle lines?

In the first verse of Psalm 8, the Hebrew which the RSV renders, "Thou whose glory above the heavens is chanted," is very awkward indeed and the translation a guess at best; while the next verse, "from the mouth of babes and infants thou hast established a stronghold because of thy foes to put to silence the vengeful enemy," does not really fit the context. Is the thought that Israel's praise puts its enemies to silence? In this praise do babes have a part? But why is revenge upon the vengeful enemy necessary? What has this to do with the theme of the Psalm? Nothing, as may be seen from the text:

Yahweh our Lord
  how majestic is thy name in all the earth! . . .
When I behold . . . the works of thy fingers,
  moon and stars which thou hast made,
What is man, that thou shouldest remember him,
  or a human being, that thou shouldest notice him,
that thou shouldest make him little less than divine
  and shouldest crown him with glory and majesty?
Thou dost make him ruler over the works of thy hands,
  all things thou hast put under his feet,
sheep and oxen, all of them,
  and moreover the wild beasts,
birds of the air and fish of the sea
  that pass along the paths through the waters.
Yahweh our Lord,
  how majestic is thy name in all the earth!

Similarly, in Psalm 16 there is a badly corrupted section near the beginning denouncing idols and those who make them, the worthless "holy ones" or god-kings on earth who deserve neither libations nor prayer. As in Psalm 8, the RSV strains to achieve good sense. In 16:11 there is a variant clause; when this and verses 3-4 are omitted or printed in small type, the basic eight-line poem stands out "with convincing clearness and commanding beauty":

Protect me, God, for in thee I take refuge,
   I say to the Lord, "Thou art my good . . .
Thou, Lord, art my proper share and my cup,
   thou dost maintain my lot."
The lines have fallen for me in fair places,
   Moreover I have a pleasant heritage.
I bless the Lord who gives me counsel;
   in the night, moreover, my conscience pricks me.
I set the Lord before me continually,
   with him at my right hand I shall not be shaken.
So my mind is glad, and my heart rejoices,
   my body, moreover, abides secure.
For thou dost not forsake me to hell,
   nor allow thy saint to see the Pit.
Thou dost show me the path of life . . .
   in thy right hand are pleasures forever.

Stanza Patterns

If the accents in a line of poetry give a clue to additions or alterations in the Psalms, enabling us, with other criteria, to discover an earlier form, is the same true of stanzas? Are there discernible four-line or six-line or other fixed stanza patterns? Despite the three poems just quoted, the evidence is not clear. Hebrew poetry in general is not strophic; it is written frequently in 10, 20, 30, 40, 50 or 70 line compositions. Because there are 22 letters in the Hebrew alphabet, 12 of the Psalms have basically 22 or a multiple of 22 lines. But, as already suggested, some 37 psalms are probably originally eight-line poems, which often fall into two four-line units, and another 25 psalms contain 12 or 16 lines.[14] Strophes or stanzas, therefore, are tantalizing; there is a temptation to look for them where perhaps in our sense of the word they did not exist. One possible reason for the common occurrence of eight-line poems is that a Hebrew scroll was about eight lines wide.

Clear patterns are to be found in Psalms 42-43 (one psalm of 30 lines with two editorial comments and a thrice-appearing refrain),[15] 49, 80, 99, and 107. In 107, for example, after a brief introducton there were once four sections of six lines each, descriptive of the classes of men who have reason to thank the Lord—travelers who have lost their way, prisoners, sick people, and sailors. Each of the four sections—until additions crept in—was similar, two lines describing the plight, two lines telling of the cry for help and its answer, then two of thanksgiving.

So the travelers (in verses 4-9):

THE PLIGHT

Those who were lost in a desolate wilderness
  finding no way to an inhabited city,
so hungry and thirsty also
  that their whole being fainted within them,

THE PLEA AND RESCUE

who cried to the Lord in their trouble
  that he would save them from their straits,

whereupon he led them by the right way
   to come to an inhabited city—

THE THANKS

let them thank the Lord for his devotion
   and for his wonderful acts for the sons of men,
for he satisfies the thirsty
   and fills the hungry with good things.

What was extraneous to this pattern was the work of an editor; the original fourth section on the sailors perhaps read simply, clearly, and rather beautifully like this:

THE PLIGHT

23. Those who embarked on the sea in ships,
    doing business on great waters,
26. Who went up to the sky, down to the depths,
    whose courage melted with misery,

THE PLEA AND RESCUE

28. who cried to the Lord in their trouble
    that he would save them from their straits,
29a. whereupon he made the storm a calm
    30b. and brought them to their desired city—

THE THANKS

31. let them thank the Lord for his devotion
    and for his wonderful acts for the sons of men,
32. and let them extol him in the congregation of people,
    and in the assembly of elders let them praise him.

When Psalm 99 is freed from four small additions, and other minor corrections made, notice the perfect symmetry between the two halves: justice balanced by forgiveness, eternal principles by actions in time, present faith by past history, the Gentiles' praise by God's revelation to Israel. The meter is probably 2:2; the refrain which first appears in lines 9 and 10 is artistically varied in 19 and 20;

The Lord reigns, let the peoples tremble,
seated on cherubim, let the earth quake.
The Lord is great in Zion
and exalted over all the peoples.
Let them praise thy name great and fearful . . .
and the might of the king who loves justice.
Thou dost establish equity, . . .
justly and virtuously thou dost act.
Extol the Lord our God
and worship at his footstool. . . .

Moses and Aaron among his priests
and Samuel with those who invoke his name
used to call to the Lord who answered them.
In the pillar of cloud he spoke to them;
they obeyed his decrees and the statute he gave them.
Lord our God thou didst answer them.
A forgiving God thou hast been to them,
forbearing to punish for their misdeeds.
Extol the Lord our God
and worship at his holy mountain. . . .

The Meaning of Selah

The problem of stanza is closely linked with that most difficult question, the meaning of *Selah*.

The Chronicler, who bears witness to the practice of the third century B.C. rather than to the time of David, tells of the Levitical singers and priest trumpeters whose duty it was "to make themselves heard in unison in praise and thanksgiving to the Lord, and when the song was raised, with trumpets and cymbals and other musical instruments, in praise to the Lord,

> 'For he is good,
> for his devotion endures for ever,'

the house, the house of the Lord, was filled with a cloud." (2 Chron. 5:12f.) Here the words

> 'For he is good,
> for his devotion endures for ever,'

appear to be a kind of praise shout, especially as another passage declares that "they sang responsively, praising and giving thanks to the Lord,

> 'For he is good
> for his devotion endures forever toward Israel.'

And all the people shouted with a great shout, when they praised the Lord." (Ezra 3:11)

The Psalms contain not only instructions for singers, but also ample evidence of praise shouts: Hallelujah (praise the Lord); praise the Lord, my soul; indeed also the same words, "for he is good, for his devotion endures for ever," which appear in the second half of each verse of Psalm 136.

Especially in Psalms 3—89, the first three-fifths of the Psalter, there are a number of varied refrains or responses suitable for choirs to sing; e.g.,

Why art thou so cast down, my soul, etc. (*Ps. 42*)
Restore us, Lord of hosts, let thy face shine
that we may be saved. (*Ps. 80*)
Be exalted, Lord, above the heavens, let thy glory
be over all the earth. (*Ps. 57*)

Besides these refrains, there are many lines loosely fitted to their contexts, urging God to arise, asserting his power to judge, invoking his protection, occasionally declaring or praying for the fidelity of his people; for example,

Arise, Lord, in thy anger, lift thyself against
the fury of my foes, and awake for me. Thou
has commanded a judgment. (*Ps. 7:6*)

O God, redeem Israel, from all his troubles.[16]

In the presence of the Lord, for he comes,
for he comes to judge the earth:
he judges the world rightly
and peoples in his faithfulness.[17]

While some of these lines may have nothing to do with a praise shout, it is possible that others may.

Selah is more likely to mean a shout of praise than *Amen* or an instrumental interlude. "Fortunate are the people who know the festal shout" (Ps. 89:15) means the people who know the proper response which it is the business of the Levites of 2 Chronicles 35:3 to teach. The "sounding cymbals" of Psalm 150:5 are the cymbals played while the people listen, the "loud clashing cymbals" (literally, the "cymbals of the festal shout") while people raise the cry of praise.

Of many possible illustrations of the use of the *Selah*, the following are instructive:

In Psalm 3, *Selah* appears at the end of verses 2, 4, and 8. The word does not occur at the end of verse 6, but instead, outside the otherwise regular metrical scheme, we find, "Arise, O Lord! Deliver me, O my God!" Is not this a clue? Is not this cry what is meant by the *Selah*?

In Psalm 9:19f, this suspicion is confirmed. Psalms 9 and 10 in Greek appear correctly as one Psalm; they contain successive letters of the alphabet at the beginning of alternate verses. At the end of Psalm 9 appears the word *Selah*, and also these lines outside the alphabetic scheme:

> "Arise, O Lord, let no man prevail,
> let the nations be judged in thy sight.
> Put fear into them, Lord,
> let the nations know that they are but men.

When the division into two Psalms was made, the editor thought it fitting to end the first with such a shout.

Psalm 46 appears in that part of the Psalter in which an attempt was made to change the divine name Yahweh or Lord into Elohim or God. Yet at verses 7 and 11 appears, "The Lord of armies is with us (Yahweh Sabaoth)." Also at verses 7 and 11, and at the end of verse 3, occurs the word *Selah*. Is it not likely that these are the words of the *Selah* appropriate to this Psalm, which at one time were omitted, or rather were indicated only by the note *Selah*, and then later restored or inserted in two places but not in the third? Here is a poem of twelve verses, made up of three equal four-line sections, with the same response at the fourth, eighth, and twelfth lines. The use of the divine name in Psalms 42—83 is frequently due to this restoration or insertion of a praise shout.

In Psalm 144:7f and 11 there is a mutilated text and curious repetition. The explanation is that a praise shout has come in from the margin to form verses 9 and 10:

> Let me sing a new song to thee, God,
> on a ten-stringed lute let me sing thy praise,
> Who dost give victory to the kings,
> who frees David his servant.

May not this be a *Selah*, although the word does not appear in the Psalm?

In Psalm 140 after the 3rd, 6th, and 9th lines the word

Selah occurs; after the 12th there appears what seems to be the *Selah* written out:

> I know that the Lord maintains
> the cause of the poor, justice for the needy.
> Surely the righteous will thank thy name;
> let the upright dwell in thy presence.

We have merely scratched the surface here of a large subject which hitherto has been a stumbling block for scholars. Will the day come when, with some degree of assurance, we may print Psalters with the praise shouts written out at the proper places for choirs, like the Levites of old, to teach the congregations to use, so that these climactic lines may ring out unequivocally, as in Psalm 56 or 59:

> In the Lord I trust, I am not afraid.
> What can flesh do to me?
>
> My strength, let me make melody to thee,
> for thou, Lord, art my fortress.

Translations Old and New

When James Moffatt was asked what part of the Bible he had translated best, he replied, "Job"; what part the worst, his reply was, "The Psalms, of course." Age after age seeks to clothe the inner thought of the psalmists in a new outer garment suited to itself, and partially succeeds, partially fails. In antiquity the Jews at Alexandria provided several

Greek dresses; that designed by Aquila was very severe and plain, unduly literal, too tight a fit, scarcely becoming. Later came models in Syriac and Latin. At every period there is uncertainty as to which garment should be worn. The worshipping community likes what is old better than what is new.

Thus the Church rejected Jerome's superb translation of the Psalms, which he made directly from the Hebrew at the end of the fourth century after fourteen years of study and writing at Bethlehem. Earlier he had revised Old Latin translations from the Greek to provide two well-worn dresses: the so-called Roman Psalter because made at Rome and for Rome, and the so-called Gallican because it first came into use in Gaul. The Gallican Psalter became too popular to be supplanted. Let us imagine a conversation between Jerome and the Western Church about the year 405.

JEROME: Mother Church, accept this present of the Scriptures which I have most carefully and accurately translated from the original tongues.

MOTHER CHURCH: Thank you, my son. In most books of the Old Testament this will be very welcome.

JEROME: Why not in all?

MOTHER CHURCH: Well, you see, in the case of the Psalter, your previous renderings are now so familiar that we can allow no change.

JEROME: But this new work of mine is based directly on the Hebrew. That old was far less accurate. It reflects the Hebrew only indirectly through the Greek and the inferior Latin of North Africans. Do you reject the better version?

MOTHER CHURCH: Yes, I'm sorry. But the Vulgate will be your translation of the Hebrew in every other Old Testament book except Psalms; in that one book, we shall keep the Gallican Psalter.

JEROME: It's a mistake, that may have serious consequences. But I shall save my translation *iuxta Hebraicam veritatem,* and perhaps some day scholars will value it.

They do!

Similarly in the seventeenth century the Church of England turned its back on the King James Version in favor of Coverdale, whose translation, made in 1535 and revised for the "Great Bible" of 1539 and 1540, Cranmer added to the first Prayer Book in 1549, whereupon it became so popular that even when the Epistles and Gospels were revised (in 1662), the old wording of the Psalms still prevailed. We may imagine a second conversation about 1611:

THE KING JAMES TRANSLATION COMMITTEE: Mother Church, accept this present of the Scriptures which we have now carefully and accurately translated from the original tongues.

THE CHURCH OF ENGLAND: Thank you, learned doctors. On the whole this will be most welcome.

THE COMMITTEE: On the whole? Why not in its entirety?

THE CHURCH: In the case of the Psalter, the Great Bible renderings are now so familiar. Besides, those older words, although less accurate, are easier to sing.

THE COMMITTEE: Should familiar rhythms be given preference over fidelity to the thought of the original?

THE CHURCH: Let's not bother with that kind of question. Anyone who wishes can look up the more accurate rendering of a Psalm in his King James Version, and the choirs can go on singing as they have for years.

THE COMMITTEE: Time makes ancient good uncouth.

THE CHURCH: Good Lord, deliver us from the sin of obsolescence, but not yet.

The Church, of course, had a certain measure of right on its side. There are passages in the Prayer Book Psalter which stand unmatched by anything in the King James or modern translations—the turns of phrase in the *Deus misereatur,* Psalm 67:

> Thy saving health among all nations—
> O let the nations rejoice and be glad;

or the surpassingly happy thanksgiving in Psalm 147:

> O praise the Lord, for it is a good thing to
> sing praises unto our God;
> Yea, a joyful and pleasant thing it is to be
> thankful.[18]

No one after drinking old wine desires new: for he says, "The old is good." (Luke 5:39)

Not only are old dresses beautiful, but the new clearly have imperfections. Dorothy Thompson made much sport of the Revised Standerd Version for its translation of Psalm 42:1, which in the King James reads: "As the hart panteth after the water brooks, so panteth my soul after thee, O God"; and in the RSV: "As a hart longs for flowing streams, so longs my soul for thee, O God." Miss Thompson's acid comment was: "A hart pants but does not long, or if he does, he can, being inarticulate, express his emotions only in some action like panting. The passionate vigor of the King James Version depends on the hart's being an animal, not a sentimental human being in a deerskin." [19]

With even more scathing criticism Dwight MacDonald in the *New Yorker* derided the RSV under the title "The Bible in Modern Undress."

Literature, and especially religious literature, is not primarily concerned with being clear and reasonable; it is connotative rather than direct, suggestive rather than explicit, decorative and incantatory rather than functional. To make the Bible readable in the modern sense means to flatten out, tone down, and convert into tepid expository prose what in the King James Version is wild, full of awe, poetic and passionate. It means stepping down the voltage of the King James Version so it won't blow any fuses. The Revisers have admirably and horribly succeeded; babes and sucklings (or infants) can play with RSV without the slightest danger of electrocution.[20]

The language they have put it into is modern expository prose, direct and clear, and also flat, insipid, and mediocre.[21]

From these criticisms two primary questions arise: was a a new translation needed in our time? and, is the RSV a worthy one? In the language of clothing, was a new dress essential if the thought of the psalmists was to circulate freely among us, and is the dress itself beautiful?

To the first of these we have already indicated the answer. The Psalms are not primarily a literary monument to be admired, but the living word of God by which his people may know him better and love him more. The RSV has given this word again to thousands. It has removed archaic and misleading expressions,[22] determined more accurately what the original writers said,[23] chosen wisely from among various possible interpretations.[24] It has substituted intelligibility for high-sounding phrases which sometimes produced a mood but did not convert experience to conscious thought.

But what of the accusation that this modern translation lacks beauty? "Tone," says Barzun, "that is the starting point . . . What effect are you producing and at what cost of words? The fewer the words, and the more transparent they are, the easier they will be to understand." [25]

One of the reasons for the difficulty in translating Hebrew is its concentration of thought. Hebrew abounds in verbs and strong, concrete nouns; it is relatively devoid of adjectives, compound words, and most of the little intermediate words that characterize many other languages. Whereas the Hebrew of Psalm 23 has fifty-five words, the English of the RSV gives just over double that number.

The translator's problem, therefore, is to avoid both a slavish literalism, stark and bare, and also unnecessary words with no direct counterpart in the original. He must supply enough to make good sense, not too many to violate the canons of simplicity, dignity, power, cadence, and rhythm.

Read aloud, then, the Revised Standard Version of Psalm 84, against the King James Version.

Ps 84 King James Version

1. How amiable are thy tabernacles, O Lord of hosts!

2. My soul longeth, yea, even fainteth for the courts of the Lord: my heart and my flesh crieth out for the living God.

3. Yea, the sparrow hath found an house, and the swallow a nest for herself, where she may lay her young, even thine altars, O Lord of hosts, my King, and my God.

4. Blessed are they that dwell in thy house: they will be still praising thee. *Selah*

5. Blessed is the man whose strength is in thee; in whose heart are the ways of them.

6. Who passing through the valley of Baca make it a well; the rain also filleth the pools.

Ps 84 RSV

1. How lovely is thy dwelling place,
   O Lord of hosts!
2. My soul longs, yea, faints
   for the courts of the Lord;
   my heart and my flesh sing for joy
   to the living God.
3. Even the sparrow finds a home
   and the swallow a nest for herself,
   where she may lay her young,
   at thy altars, O Lord of hosts,
   my king and my God.
4. Blessed are those who dwell in thy house,
   ever singing thy praise! *Selah*
5. Blessed are the men whose strength is in thee,
   in whose heart are the highways to Zion.
6. As they go through the valley of Baca
   they make it a place of springs;
   the early rain also covers it with pools.

Ps 84 King James Version (continued)

7. They go from strength to strength, every one of them in Zion appeareth before God.
8. O Lord God of hosts, hear my prayer: give ear, O God of Jacob. *Selah*
9. Behold, O God our shield, and look upon the face of thine anointed.
10. For a day in thy courts is better than a thousand. I had rather be a doorkeeper in the house of my God, then to dwell in the tents of wickedness.

11. For the Lord God is a sun and shield: the Lord will give grace and glory: no good thing will he withhold from them that walk uprightly.

12. O Lord of hosts, blessed is the man that trusteth in thee.

Ps 84 RSV (continued)

7. They go from strength to strength;
   the God of gods will be seen in Zion.
8. O Lord God of hosts, hear my prayer:
   give ear, O God of Jacob. *Selah*
9. Behold our shield, O God;
   look upon the face of thine anointed!
10. For a day in thine courts is better
    than a thousand elsewhere.
    I would rather be a doorkeeper in the house of my God
    than dwell in the tents of wickedness.
11. For the Lord God is a sun and shield;
    he bestows favor and honor.
    No good thing does the Lord withhold
    from those who walk uprightly.
12. O Lord of hosts,
    blessed is the man who trusts in thee!

Are the cadences of the RSV inferior to those of the King James? However much one may like the word "amiable," "lovely" is a distinct improvement for twentieth century readers. "Ever singing thy praise" is less cumbersome than "they will be still praising thee." "Highways to Zion" makes sense where "in whose heart are the ways of them" does not, although in this case "in whose heart are pilgrimages," and even "in whose mind are songs of praise" are perhaps preferable renderings. "Everyone of them in Zion appeareth before God" should read "that they may see the Lord in Zion," but "the God of gods will be seen in Zion" is at least a step in the right direction. In the KJ phrase "Behold, O God our shield" there lurks an ambiguity which is now removed; it is clear that the shield is the anointed one and not God, and the RSV properly reads "Behold our shield, O God." The shift of "the Lord" from the second to the third line of verse 11 improves the rhythm, and the use of the word "elsewhere" in verse 10 both makes the meaning clearer and rounds out the poetic line. This translation may be further improved,[26] but even now is the equal of any other in English, in some respects clearly superior.

Traditional Vocabulary or Greater Intelligibility?

For the modern reader, in a changing age, one of the chief problems of the Psalms is their so-called religious vocabulary. This is true for two reasons: on the one hand, the words may be so difficult as to repel him from this literature altogether; on the other, they may be so soothing that they lull him to slumber in a false piety. Words such as *truth, grace, peace, judgment, righteousness,* and *salvation* may have become so vague, so remote from their original tangible meanings, as to provide the worshipper with the satisfactions of godliness without even a prick of conscience over departure from what they were intended to signify.

Shall then a modern translation give up these words, so rich in time-honored association, for substitutes that may have misleading connotations of their own? Or shall a special biblical terminology be avoided at all costs? Even if our sympathies are with those who would bring religion out of the sanctuary into the market place, the practical decision over word after word must continue to plague the translator.

For example, in the RSV the older *salvation* has frequently been changed to *victory, victories* or *help.*[27] But would not "thou God of my salvation" (Ps. 51:14) be rendered better as "God my helper" or "God who rescues me"? "The glad sense of thy help" is what "the joy of thy salvation" first expressed. Sometimes, thus, the older word is removed, sometimes retained. Or again, *host* (Ps. 27:3) means *army* rather than a multitude, and *war* in the same verse a *hostile band.* "He makes wars cease" (Ps. 46:9) refers to the elimination of enemy armies. But there is much understandable resistance to the loss of traditional language in passages such as these.

Because in the sixteenth century "evil" meant both moral evil and physical harm, it is confusing to retain *evil* in the passages where it means only harm. "When I walk through the gloomy valley, I fear no harm." [28] For "the Lord will preserve thee from all evil," the modern idiom might be, "the Lord will protect you from all harm." *Preserve* does not equal *guard* or *protect;* and keep—another traditional rendering—today means "to retain." [29] Especially misleading is the word *soul* with all its associations that are alien to the psalmists themselves. It stands for *self* or *life,* or sometimes *desire,* and no one translation of the Hebrew word is adequate. Thus, "The law of the Lord is perfect, restoring life," (Ps. 19:7) or "who does not exert himself wrongfully." (Ps. 24:4) But how best to avoid *soul* in such expressions as "Bless the Lord, O my soul" remains a problem. It is unfortunate that the RSV, which removed the word from Psalm 16:10 ("Thou dost not give me up to Sheol") should introduce it where it had not been before in the previous verse.

Should proper names like Sheol and Leviathan be kept? *Sheol* is not readily understood, *hell* misleading. If Sheol is kept, then should the technical word *Negeb* be substituted for *South:* "Restore our fortunes, O Lord, like the water-courses in the Negeb"? (Ps. 126:4) Is it not better in general to employ terms that are clear without elaborate explanation; e.g., to recognize a crocodile when he is mentioned, and not to hide him behind Leviathan? (Ps. 104:26)

The longer one studies problems of this kind, the more he

realizes their complexity and the less he is inclined to dogmatize. He will not lightly avoid terms around which precious connotations have gathered. On the whole, the reader who has a passion for understanding will suffer some losses for the sake of greater intelligiblity. *Mercy,* for example, brings to the modern mind something quite other than the Hebrew intends, which is *affectionate loyalty* or *devotion,* fidelity in a personal relationship based on love. *Loving kindness* is too mild, *leal-love* good for Scotland but not the U.S.A., *steadfast love* redundant in expressions like "his steadfast love endures."

The answer, therefore, to the problem as to whether the distinctly Biblical diction should be retained or the use of older terminology be replaced by words of everyday currency is a both/and answer rather than an either/or. The King James and Prayer Book versions of the Psalms will surely continue to hold unchallenged positions in the English speaking world. But the argument of this chapter has been that the old is not enough.

> "They must upward still and onward
> who would keep abreast of truth."

Or, to revert to our earlier metaphor, the production of new dresses must always continue.

Imagine, therefore, a third conversation between the Christian community and an individual scholar or group of translators and reinterpreters such as the Revised Standard Version Committee:

THE SCHOLARS: Christians of the twentieth century, here are Psalms in the English spoken in the United States in our time.

CHRISTIANS: Does this translation threaten the Prayer Book and King James versions?

THE SCHOLARS: Hardly. If history gives any indication, they will always have places of honor among translations of the Psalms.

CHRISTIANS: Why then should we read your work?

THE SCHOLARS: By being open to the full force of the ancient expressions, you will discern more clearly the word of life.

CHRISTIANS: But literary experts make sport of your flaws, and those who take you most seriously burn copies of your translations.

THE SCHOLARS: The burnings provide much valuable advertising. But we know perhaps better than anyone else that our work is imperfect, only a new dress that will give way to another.

CHRISTIANS: Then isn't this the Word of God?

THE SCHOLARS: Read it and see!

V.

COMING ALIVE TODAY

"When they had sung a hymn, they went out to the Mount of Olives." (Mark 14:26) [1] "Be filled with the Spirit . . . in psalms and hymns and spiritual songs, singing and making melody in your heart to the Lord." (Eph. 5:18, 19)

In the back of our minds is the recollection that the Psalms were staple diet in the spiritual nourishment of our Lord and even of the early Church that broke away from Judaism. There are 116 quotations from the Psalms in the New Testament, more than from any other book, two-fifths of all the Old Testament quotations in the New. A study like Prothero's *The Psalms in Human Life,* or Marson's *The Psalms at Work,* is hardly required to remind us how down through the ages these poems have strengthened Jews and Christians in difficulty, comforted them in sorrow, given them courage in death, guided them in life. But the question we have been considering is whether they can speak to this wealthy nation. If so, in this final chapter it remains to inquire how to use them most effectively.

Immediately we disclaim any thought of manipulating this literature to create a mood or produce effects. If we agree with Joseph Sittler that there are five elements which characterize Christian worship in all its major forms: recollection, thanksgiving, participation, proclamation, and expectation,[2] the Psalms assist at all points; but we are seeking not so much to use them as that they may come alive in us. What we deplore is that they should be a hindrance rather than a help for many who try to worship—even for many a minister, for he, too, finds the Psalms a traditional form of worship with which he does not quite know how to cope. He gives out a psalm because the tradition prompts him to say something, not because he is convinced that the psalm has something vital to say.

The Whole Psalter?

The first problem with which he must deal is whether he will attempt to use all of the Psalter. In the Prayer Book of the Episcopal Church, the Psalter is divided into sections for thirty mornings and thirty evenings with the expectation that it will be read in its entirety each month. English parsons, who are bound to read Morning and Evening Prayer daily, continue this practice. But one may confess to a degree of scepticism over this method, especially when it is used at jet-plane speed. One reason is that the sections for our people are mostly too long. A certain woman found herself the only member of the congregation on the fifteenth evening one month, when she and the curate bandied back and forth 73 verses of the 78th Psalm. She did not return to mid-week evensong and henceforth avoided the curate and the Psalm. Better "five words with my mind, in order to instruct others, than ten thousand words in a tongue," (1 Cor. 14:19) and perhaps, more than we are ready to admit, the Psalter is for our people a speaking in tongues. A second and more important reason, however, is that the Psalms are so uneven in their range from the worst to the best in man's heart. Mr. C.S. Lewis defends with all the skill of which he is so capable the use of the imprecatory psalms.[3] It is true that if we are to advance from milk to meat we must be prepared for gristle, and I would not advocate the abandonment of any great record of man's experience solely because of its difficulty. Some roughage in our diet is acceptable enough, but not wide tracts of psalms which are both hard to comprehend and still harder to reconcile with the New Testament when comprehended.

As an alternative, we use a lectionary of psalms such as that in the front of the Prayer Book, and even within this selection, build for ourselves a working list of psalms that we may call our own. The late Archbishop Temple mentions his favorites in this order: 103, 23, 104, 107, 139, 126, 130, 51; then 84, 90, 16, 46, 137, 19. He omits a few which are generally treasured as not his particular meat: Psalms 8, 27, 42, 43, 121, 24, 91, 100, and 145.[4] Whoever keeps records of psalms especially loved by many groups is likely to find that there are roughly fifty which are highly prized, fifty which few would stoutly defend, and fifty which in some parts or for some people are capable of inclusion in their working Psalter. Within the first fifty, about twenty-five stand out above the rest. Even though these may vary in importance for various individuals, is it not desirable to have a relatively short list on which we can rely because we have, to some important extent, grasped what the psalmist declares and shared in the thought and feeling which he there expresses? Unless the leaders of worship have progressed this far, it will be more difficult for the congregation to hear more than the words. This does not mean that we slough off two-thirds of the Psalter; rather, that we resolve not to use the psalms mechanically, but with purpose and skill and intelligence and knowledge to make the most of their place in divine worship, and from a core of well-known favorites to be reaching out constantly into other psalms which one by one become ours and others' also.

Advent Psalms

To illustrate this method, we propose to glance at some of the psalms suggested for the Sundays of Advent, Quinquagesima, and Lent. Can we detect why certain psalms have been chosen for certain days? What do they contribute to the worship of those days? As we use them, what will help us to "sing praises with understanding"? (Ps. 47:7 BCP)

For the First Sunday in Advent, the morning psalms are 50, 46, and 97. As Psalm 50 has been discussed in Chapter

I and a brief exposition of the meaning of Psalm 46 will follow (see p. 130), their relevance to the beginning of a penitential season and a new Christian Year needs no further comment here.

But why has Psalm 97 been chosen? The Gospel for the day, from Matthew 21, presents the triumphal entry of the Lord into Jerusalem. In the beginning, the Church foresees the end when he who is meek shall also "be exalted far above all gods" and receive the acclaim: Hosanna in the highest. Psalm 97 emphatically declares this message that "The Lord is King"; God rules and, in ruling, rescues and blesses the upright. As in the Palm Sunday story, so here multitudes rejoice. The gospel's reference to one that "comes in the name of the Lord" reflects the psalm's "remembrance of his holiness," which is a Hebrew way of saying "his holy name." The God who reigns is not to be welcomed lightly; he is the Lord of righteousness and justice who upsets the tables, and the plans, of all that delight in vain gods. "Sion" appears in both psalm and gospel (the "daughters" in the former probably refer not exclusively to women, but to the inhabitants of Jerusalem's surrounding towns).

Finally, what is more appropriate for the beginning of Advent, when we "put upon us the armour of light," than the declaration that light dawns—in one reading, *is sown;* in another, *rises*—for the "true-hearted"?

The Second Sunday in Advent is "Bible Sunday," for which the morning psalms suggested are 25 and 119:1-16.

Fortunate are those whose way is blameless,
Who walk by the law of the Lord.

(*Cf. Matt.* 5:48.)

Fortunate are those who observe his decrees,
Who seek him whole-heartedly . . .
How can a young man stay pure?
By keeping thy word . . .
In my mind I treasure thy promise.
That I may not sin against thee . . .
In thy statutes I find joy;
I forget not thy word.

Surely here, in this 119th Psalm, the point is not the artificial arrangement, the details of which one may read in any commentary, but the delight of the student of God's Word.

Similarly Psalm 25, although written in inferior Hebrew, repetitious, and hampered to some extent by its alphabetical arrangement, makes important affirmations about God's law. The argument of this psalm is as follows: because the Lord's pity and devotion are "unfailing through the ages" (v. 5 BCP), he teaches his way or his *torah* or law to his humble worshippers (vv. 3, 7-9, 11), saving them from their sins (vv. 6, 10, 17), freeing them from the tensions, the traps, and the distresses that afflict them both within and without (vv. 2, 14-18), protecting their integrity (vv. 8, 20), and granting security. Their descendants will possess the Holy Land (v. 12). Notice the distinction between the sinful self and the true self ("remember not the sins of my youth . . . remember me"; v. 6). Especially memorable is the assertion that "those who worship the Lord are in his confidence," or, as verse 13 might also be rendered, "Intimacy with the Lord is granted to his worshippers, and theirs is the revelation of his covenant."

Had the author's ability to express the truth matched the truth which he wished to express, this 25th Psalm might have had a high place among the psalms. His lack was partially redeemed by the early English translators, whose power of phrasing occasionally reached great heights. Consider, for example, the Prayer Book Version of the verse last mentioned ("The secret of the Lord is among them that fear him"); or verse 5, "Call to remembrance, O Lord, thy tender mercies, and thy loving kindnesses which have been ever of old"; or another verse (9) particularly appropriate to this Bible Sunday, "All the paths of the Lord are mercy and truth unto such as keep his covenant and his testimonies."

For the Third Sunday, when the Church considers its ministry, the morning psalms are 22:23-32, 99, 85, and 107:1-16. (For comment on the three latter see pp. 87, 19ff., and 85ff. respectively.) The latter part of Psalm 22 is appropriate because, as John the Baptist prepares the Lord's way, so the psalm speaks of the Lord's generation "that shall come to declare his righteousness." As through the Lord the poor have the gospel preached to them, so in the psalm

"The poor shall eat and be satisfied;
they that seek after the Lord shall praise him."
(Ps. 22:26 BCP; cf. v. 24.)

The end of this psalm, like the beginning, is preserved only in a badly damaged text which needs careful study. In verse 29, for example (Hebrew v. 30) the word translated *have eaten* should probably be divided into two words: *him alone* the prosperous on earth—by which is meant earth's rulers—are to worship. The chief themes, however, are plain: joy and thanksgiving for God's care of the afflicted; remembrance of God that leads to repentance and universal worship; acknowledgment of his rule and the proclamation of his reign of righteousness "unto a people that shall be born." (Cf. Ps. 78:1-4.)

Psalm 100, one of the three appointed for the morning of the Fourth Sunday in Advent, is a favorite vehicle of praise for both Jews and Christians. As the *Jubilate,* the canticle to follow the second lesson in Morning Prayer, it is perhaps in less than the best place, for it is an invitation to serve the Lord and a reminder of how to approach him. In other words, the habit of singing at the beginning of a service the paraphrases of this Psalm—William Kethe's "All people that on earth do dwell," and Isaac Watt's "From all that dwell below the skies"—is sound liturgical practice. As the title (a Psalm for the thank offering) suggests a Jewish rite with a tangible gift, so "serve the Lord" suggests action as well as word, and "thanksgiving" (v. 3 BCP) might be translated "thank offering." Where the written text reads *and not we ourselves* (v. 2), the spoken text and early versions preferred "and we are his," a rendering which fits better the following line and the concept of election which underlies this psalm. The Lord *made* his people in order to form with them a bond which endures forever for the *sheep of his pasture,* i.e., the nation which acknowledges or *knows,* by association with the Lord, that he is God.

On the eve of Christmas, therefore, come before the Lord with joy, proclaiming his sovereign goodness, with an offering of thanks and praise, with a gift that is more than lip service, and with trust in his abiding faithfulness.

Let the beautiful Psalm 80 speak for itself. For Christians, although not for Jews, the man of God's right hand is the Christ, at whose coming the vine revives, in the light of whose face his people are saved. Two verses are omitted; the refrains are made to read identically.

O Shepherd of Israel, give ear,
  Thou who dost lead Joseph like a flock!
Thou who dost sit on the cherubim, shine forth
  before Ephraim and Benjamin and Manasseh.
Awaken thy mighty power
  and come to save us!
Lord of hosts, restore us
  and let thy face shine that we may be saved.

Lord of hosts, how long
  wilt thou be angry with thy people's prayer?
Thou hast fed them with the bread of woe,
  and given them tears to drink in abundance.
Thou dost make us a laughing stock to our neighbors
  and our enemies ridicule us.

Lord . . . of hosts, restore us
  and let thy face shine that we may be saved.

A vine thou didst remove from Egypt,
  thou didst drive out nations and plant it in;
Thou didst clear a way before it,
  and it took root and filled the land.
Mountains were covered with its shade
  and mighty cedars with its branches.
[Lord . . . of hosts, restore us,
  and let thy face shine that we may be saved.]

It extended its boughs to the sea
  and its shoots to the River.
Why hast thou broken down its walls
  so that all who pass by can pluck it?
The boar from the forest gnaws at it,
  and the wild creatures graze upon it.
Lord of hosts, restore [us
  and let thy face shine that we may be saved.]

Look down from heaven and see
  and take notice of this vine. . . .
Let thy hand be on the man of thy right hand,
  on the son of man whom thou didst rear for thyself.
Then shall we not turn back from thee;
  revive us that we may call on thy name.
Lord . . . of hosts, restore us
  and let thy face shine that we may be saved.

The Sunday Before Lent

For Quinquagesima, when we read as the Epistle the thirteenth chapter of I Corinthians and repeat in the collect that "all our doings without charity are nothing worth," the theme is love, "the ultimate ideal of Christian life." Psalms, hymns, and lessons may all be chosen in such a way as to reinforce it. As the minister prepares, perhaps reading Massey Shepherd's *Oxford American Prayer Book Commentary*, he will notice that among the psalms appointed for the day are 23 and 103, and that the same commentary contains notes on both of these.[5]

As for Psalm 103, would it be helpful to point out the steps in the psalm's structural development noted in Chapter II, or at least call attention to the picture of the tent formed by God's love over all his worshippers? A note in the leaflet connecting collect, epistle, lesson, hymns, and psalm would show that there was a good reason for the selections this day and redeem the service from dull conventionality or any reproach of having been carelessly prepared.

If Psalm 23 is to be used, the bulletin might also indicate that the so-called Shepherd Psalm has not only this one metaphor for which it is named, but also another, that of God as Host. The Shepherd provides pasturage and refreshing water (at wells probably rather than brooks); he restores life to his sheep, guides them on right paths, and when danger threatens and the valley is dark and frightening, protects and comforts them. The Host provides a banquet. Even when enemies are near they are not dangerous, for the Lord's bounty and devotion—covering man's head with the oil, which symbolizes honoring a guest with more than bare necessities of life, filling his cup full to the brim—pursue him all the days of his life and give him security in the Temple to the end of time. Notice the national implication in the reference to the Lord's house; Israel makes this its home.

Here, just before Lent begins, is the declaration of God's providence, refreshment, guidance, care, generosity, and devotion. The coming season is not a time to be painfully endured, for it promises renewed appreciation of God's love and communion with him. It invites us to a better community. In the teaching of Jesus there is a double strain. He bids men follow him when he has no place to lay his head, but also to come to him to find rest.

Lenten Psalms

Not all the Sundays provide such a wealth of material. Psalms 23, 103, and 139 (which last is suggested for the evening of Quinquagesima) are the most precious of the whole collection. But because it is a method which we are illustrating, let us continue on to the First Sunday in Lent. The theme of the collect, epistle, and gospel is fasting or, more broadly, self-discipline, abstinence, the endurance of affliction and temptation that the flesh may be subdued to the Spirit. Among the psalms appointed for the day are 50, which we discussed in the first chapter, and 15, sometimes called the "Ten Commandments of the Psalter." Neither of these was included in the list of the favorites. Psalm 15 is hardly a psalm at all, for it is not a hymn of praise; it is not a declaration of trust in the midst of suffering. It is rather an answer to the question, "Who may come into God's tent?" or "Who belongs in the circle of those who live in favor with God?" The affluent society is bidden to remember the difference between the ways of the world and the ways of the Kingdom. In the form of a code, the commandments of this psalm might read thus:

1. You shall keep the law. The person who walks blamelessly, who leads the incorrupt life, is the one whose conduct is perfect because he strictly obeys the commands of God.
2. You shall speak truth. *From the heart* or *sincerely* may mean either *willingly, gladly,* or with no difference between thought and word.
3. You shall not slander a neighbor. The word for *used no deceit* is connected with the word for *foot*—you shall not patter about gossiping.
4. You shall not harm a friend.
5. You shall not hurt the good name of your kin.
6. You shall loathe the godless: "Pompous arrogance he despises" (the Prayer Book follows a different reading: "He that setteth not by himself, but is lowly in his own eyes").

7. You shall honor the worshippers of the Lord—to *honor* (*make much of*) is to *approve, choose, associate with.*

8. You shall keep your promises—even if harmful to your own interests.

9. You shall not take advantage of another's misfortune—for in the ancient Jewish world not only exorbitant interest, but the lending of money for gain was forbidden. Money was lawfully loaned only for the relief of distress.

10. You shall shun bribery—one of the most common sins condemned also in the law and the prophets.

In sum, of these commandments the first two (v. 2 BCP) deal with right action and right intent before God; 3, 4, and 5 (v. 3 BCP) with speech and action toward fellow men (perhaps in an ascending scale of nearness); 6 and 7 (v. 4 BCP) with the proper relation to those who do not or do worship God; and 8, 9, and 10 (*vv.* 5, 6 BCP) with right behavior particularly in money matters.

It may be charged that most of these commands are couched negatively, that they neglect some of the worst sins, and that they are neither especially comprehensive nor profound. But, at the beginning of Lent, the prosperous American congregation may not improperly test itself to see whether it has progressed at least this far. God distinguishes an Israel within Israel, those of whom he can approve because they meet his conditions, who as they worship learn to do what is right and therefore are secure. This should be an easy psalm for any congregation to understand, sufficiently difficult for all to practise.

For the Second Sunday in Lent, which has no such distinct theme as the first, one of the psalms appointed is Psalm 30,[6] which we have already discussed. For the Third Sunday the very beautiful Psalm 27 is appointed. If the minister has been printing in a bulletin comments on the Psalms, this week for variety and on the theory that a good translation is the best commentary, he might present a modern version which brings out the literal meaning of many words that customarily slip by unheeded:

The Lord is my light and my aid;
  Whom shall I fear?
The Lord is the stronghold of my life;
  of whom shall I be afraid?
When evildoers assail me
  to devour my flesh,[7]
My foes and my enemies,
  they stumble and fall.
Although an army encamp against me,
  my heart does not fear,
Although a battle-line rise against me,
  even then I am confident.
One thing I ask of the Lord,
  that do I seek: . . .
to behold the beauty of the Lord
  and to contemplate his temple.
For he hides me in his shelter
  on the day of trouble,
he conceals me under the cover of his tent,

on a rock he sets me high.
Now therefore my head is exalted
over my enemies around me,
That I may offer in his tent
sacrifices with resounding joy. . . .
Lord, hear my voice when I cry,
pity me and answer me.
My mind has spoken for thee,
"Seek my face."
Thy face, Lord, do I seek,
do not hide from me!
Do not cast off thy servant in anger.
thou hast been my help;
Do not abandon nor forsake me,
my God, who comes to my aid!
Although my father and mother forsake me,
the Lord cares for me.
Teach me thy way, Lord,
and lead me on a level path
because of my lurking enemies.
Do not give me over
to the will of my foes,
For false witnesses have risen against me,
snorting violence.
I believe I shall see the goodness of the Lord
in the land of the living . . .
Be strong and let your heart take courage
and wait for the Lord!

The controlling theme here is the search for God through Temple, Torah, and Trust, and it leads to deliverance, dedication, and delight.

Two of the Psalms for the Fourth Sunday in Lent, 46 and 122, are discussed in Dr. Case's useful little manual, *Seven Psalms*;[8] for the Fifth Sunday there is the magnificent 51st, or if something has been said about that on Ash Wednesday, the 42nd-43rd, which are to be taken together as one psalm, and also the difficult but rewarding 40th. If on Palm Sunday Psalm 22 is to be used, careful study is essential, nothing less; other possibilities are 130 or 24 or 97. There is no dearth of excellent psalms for the Easter season. By studying, expounding, illustrating them one by one, this part of public worship may come alive.

Inexhaustible Mines of Lore

As was suggested earlier, a vast amount of lore connected with the Psalms is available upon which to draw to stimulate interest. I mention here only three relatively accessible sources.

First there is the connection between psalms and hymns. Upwards of thirty hymns in *The Hymnal, 1940,* are based on psalms; the connection is worth tracing out. If in these days it is highly important to avoid soft sentimentality and to use hymns of an "objective" type in which personal pronouns are few while great affirmations about God are many, here are some of the best, all based on Psalms:

All people that on earth do dwell; (*Psalm 100*)
The spacious firmament on high; (*19*)
A mighty fortress is our God; (*46*)
Praise my soul the King of Heaven; (*103*)
Hail to the Lord's Anointed; (72)
O worship the King, all glorious above; (*104*) and
O God our help in ages past. (*90*)

We sometimes smile at the Scottish paraphrases:

Blessed shall that trooper be
  Who, riding on his naggie,
Takes thy bairns with muckle glee
  and dashes them on the craggie." (*137*)

We do not intend to turn the clock back to the time when hymns other than psalms were uncommon. But what lies behind the insistence on the part of some Calvinistic groups that the Psalms, after all, are the proper vehicle of the Church's praise? Why was it said, "The Psalms are flagons, hymns are only the cups"?

Second, there is no end of interest in the comparison of various English versions of the Psalms. We have just seen how Prayer Book and other versions diverge in Psalm 15; the 23rd is another conspicuous example. In that 23rd Psalm notice the marginal notes in the Revised Standard Version. Although the King James is more accurate than the Prayer Book, and generally the translators of the RSV seek a higher degree of fidelity to the Hebrew than the

King James, in this case the traditional renderings were too firmly embedded in popular affection to be dislodged, and the more faithful reproduction of the sense of the original is to be obtained only through the margin. When this psalm is read, there is a good opportunity to develop the meaning of some of the basic words, such as *goodness* and *mercy*, or *soul*.

Sixteenth-century translations, if available, provide an abundant mine for an enriched appreciation of various verses. These examples are taken from a Matthew Bible of 1549:

> At the last, I came to this point, that I thought:
> O why art thou so foolish: the right hand of the most highest can change all. (*Ps.* 77)
>
> I will take no wicked thing in hand,
> I hate the sin of unfaithfulness . . .
> Whoso hath a proud look and an high stomach,
> I may not away with him. (*Ps. 101*)
>
> So shall I spy out wondrous things in thy law.
> (*Ps. 119:31*)
>
> I stick unto thy testimonies. (*Ps. 119:14*)
>
> Thy loving correction maketh me great.
> Thou hast made room enough under me for to go.
> (*Ps. 18:35*f.)
>
> Thy staff and thy sheephook comfort me. (*Ps.* 23)

Third, the use of other languages is a never-failing aid as we attempt to fathom the meaning of expressions in our own. These few references are indicative of the stimulus of the Latin:

Quare . . . populi meditantur inania?
(*Ps. 2:1*)
Mane propono tibi precas meas et expecto.
(*Ps. 5:4; Ps. 5:3 RSV*)
Beatus populus qui exultare novit.
(*Ps. 88:16; Ps. 89:15 RSV*)
Aspicite ad eum, ut exhilaremini.
(*Ps. 33:6; Ps. 34:5 RSV*)
Securi sint qui diligunt te.
(*Ps. 121:6; Ps. 122 RSV*)
Ascensiones in corde suo disposuit.
(*Ps. 83:6; Ps. 84:5 RSV*)
Ipse enim novit abscondita cordis.
(*Ps. 43:22; Ps. 44:21 RSV*)
In aeternum non vacillabit.
(*Ps. 111:6; Ps. 112 RSV*)

St. Jerome translated the Hebrew of Psalm 51:14 (*51:12* RSV): *Redde mihi laetitiam Jesu tui* (restore to me the joy of thy Jesus); and again Psalm 150:1, Praise the Lord in his holy one, that is Christ. The Old Latin of our Psalm 96:10 (BCP), "Tell it out among the heathen that the Lord is King," included the words *a ligno,* from a tree, i.e., from the

Cross. Although Justin Martyr was wrong in charging the Jews with having removed these words from their text, the hymn *Vexilla Regis,* written by Venantius Fortunatus about 600, preserves the memory of that Old Latin reading:

> Fulfilled is now what David told
> In true prophetic song of old,
> How God the heathen's king should be,
> For God is reigning from the tree.

Truly the lore is endless. What is a shawm, of which we sing so often in Evening Prayer's canticle, the 98th Psalm? It is a reed instrument of the oboe class, but the Hebrew refers to a ram's horn (shofar). How did some Bibles come to be called "Bugges Bibles"? Because in Psalm 91:5 these read, for *terror* of the night, *bogies,* spelled b-u-g-g-e-s, "thou shalt not need to be afraid for any bugges by night." Why is a late second-century date probable for Psalm 2? Because the initial letters of the first ten lines spell, "To Jannaeus and his wife" (Alexandra) who were married in 103 B.C. In that same psalm, how are we to interpret the words: "And rejoice with trembling. Kiss son"? We do as the RSV translators did, transpose the Hebrew letters, and obtain excellent sense, "With trembling kiss his feet."

So on *ad infinitum.* But if what we were saying in the earlier chapters about the new requirements of a new day is valid, then we shall keep a proper balance between meat and spice; and the main thrust of our teaching and explaining will be to uncover the psalmists' essential experiences and basic presuppositions, their great affirmations and their grasp of life's essential issues.

Preaching from the Psalms

In the foregoing we have given abundant indication of how the Psalms may provide many a theme for preaching, and offer permanent pictorial expressions of eternal truth. But with some hesitation, since I am not now in charge of a parish and preaching Sunday after Sunday, I put forth a suggestion about the early celebration of the Holy Communion. In the preface to *The Crown of the Year,* Dr. Austin Farrer says:

It is an old dilemma, that a sermon at a said eucharist destroys the special character of a simple rite, whereas "no sermon" leaves the communicants without assistance and divorces the sacrament from the word. In a college chapel, where ears are somewhat quicker than elsewhere, it is possible to avoid both evils, the priest can read out in place of a sermon a written paragraph of his own no longer than the gospel for the day. Whether such a practice could be adapted to the needs of parish congregations, I do not profess to know; but I should strongly hold that, whatever modifications might be introduced for their benefit, neither a material expansion of length, nor the substitution of free speech for a written text ought to be contemplated.[9]

Here are two attempts at such paragraphs, one which deals with the problem of special providence raised in the Gospel for the First Sunday in Lent by the words of the 91st

Psalm which the tempter quoted: "If thou be the Son of God, cast thyself down: for it is written, He shall give his angels charge over concerning thee: and in their hands they shall bear thee up, lest at any time thou dash thy foot against a stone."

> Our Lord rebuffs Satan, even though the latter quotes Scripture to his purpose. For the Lord looks behind the literal face value of the words to their essential meaning. Did the psalmist literally believe that the hands of God's angels would lift men above their difficulties, or that the people he addressed were likely to step on a lion or would never stub their toes? Does God's care exempt his chosen from the miseries that are the common lot of mankind? Do not his sun and rain fall on the just and unjust alike? Is the psalmist then wrong? Like St. Paul, he is a deceiver who is yet true. Make allowance for poetic heightening. He is wrong in that he appears to deny that physical hurt can come to the believer. Jesus did not escape the Cross. But both psalmist and the Lord are right in making God their refuge and fortress, in trusting, in loving, and in finding that in the end God does answer, deliver, and bring to honor.

A paragraph on Psalm 46, for the First Sunday in Advent, might run like this:

> One of the proper Psalms for this day, the 46th, fortifies us for the new year. Everything may seem to be in

commotion, as even in the natural order the earth quakes, mountains shake on their foundation and the seas roar and foam, while among men nations rage and kingdoms totter. But if many cities of the world are only inadequately defended by rivers, God's Jerusalem has the power of her Lord streaming forth fully to protect her. He is our refuge and our stronghold, a well tried help in trouble. It is he whose work is to make wars cease. Right early, at the turn of the morning, he is with us, bidding all who oppose him to desist. They cannot win. And those who acknowledge that he is exalted over the nations, exalted over the earth, have nothing to fear from the turbulence of today or of the year ahead. The eternal God is their mighty fortress.

If the minister is accustomed to preach both at an early and late service on Sunday morning, does this suggestion offer a way of improvement?

Praying Through the Psalms

Having risked one suggestion that may have little value for our American scene, let me venture another that may possess more. We hear frequently that we need "to think biblically." If that means to use a language all our own, we shall have nothing to do with it. If it means to substitute half-understood terms for words that can convey clear meaning, we shun it. We cannot recover the life of two thousand years ago, nor do we wish to. But if biblical thinking means a serious effort to understand and express what the ancient writers were saying, if it means we shall listen humbly to their pictorial poetry, then indeed we need to think with the biblical authors, and not least the psalmists.

Again, the *lex orandi* is the *lex credendi.* Then let us try to put a few of the Psalms into the form of collects suitable for use at the close of a service in which the psalm has already been read.

> O God, who hast done great things for us whereof we are glad, who hast filled our mouth with laughter and our tongue with singing, teach us also that they who sow in tears shall reap in joy, and grant that we who go forth to plant the good seed of thy Son the Sower, whether thy service makes us happy or makes us sad, may come home rejoicing when he brings in his sheaves, through the same Jesus Christ our Lord. (*Based on Ps. 126.*)

> O God, the Judge of all the peoples and the Governor of every nation upon earth, who through no merit of ours hast prospered our land and given us a rich increase of wealth and peace, grant us grace to make known thy way upon earth, thy saving health among all nations, until all peoples praise thee and every man is blessed, through Jesus Christ our Lord. (*Based on Ps. 67.*)

O Lord, our eternal dwelling place, who art our God from everlasting to everlasting, we remember that our lives pass as a watch in the night; we acknowledge our iniquities that are open to all and the secret sins that are revealed in the light of thy countenance. As all our pride is dust, so teach us to count our days that we may find wisdom for the work thou hast called us to do, and so satisfy us with thy love that we may rejoice and be glad all our days in thy service, through Jesus Christ our Lord. (*Based on Ps. 90.*)

O God, who makest us glad when we go to thy house, where pilgrims gather to give thee thanks with all the tribes of thy people, hear our prayer for the peace of thy cities and for the prosperity of all thy children out of every race and nation; and grant, for our brethren and companion's sakes, that we may seek and labor for the good of thy Kingdom, through Jesus Christ our Lord. (*Based on Ps. 122.*)

This last is reminiscent of another prayer. Dr. Case, in her *Seven Psalms,*[10] uses a quotation from Dionysius the Carthusian, who died in 1471, which she had picked up from a source she could no longer identify. I had been eager to find it for many years; then one day as I sat in an alcove of St. Deiniol's Library, Hawarden, Chester, England, I reached up and took down a commentary on the Psalms by this Dionysius, published by Peter Quentelli of Cologne in 1545. At the end of the section on Psalm 121 (in our numbering 122), there were the Latin words which, in English, Miss Case had quoted thus: "O God, the artificer of all things which be, cause our feet to stand in thy courts; build up within us Jerusalem which is above; let us have unbroken peace in thy might, that we may always seek the good of that same city, and may find it by thine aid." [11]

The Use of the Psalms in the Pastoral Ministry

Finally, even in a prosperous age the Church has a never-ending pastoral ministry to the sick and to the bereaved, to prisoners and refugees, to the aged and lonely, to self-haters and those who have never learned to accept and give love. There is no guarantee that another period of war and woe may be long postponed, but in all time of our prosperity as in all time of our tribulation, the Church's pastoral duty never ceases. In this part of her total work, she possesses an invaluable resource in the Psalms.

For the psalmists have themselves suffered. "The very angels themselves," says Thornton Wilder, "cannot persuade the wretched and blundering children on earth as can one human being broken on the wheels of living. In Love's service only the wounded can serve." [12]

Some of the Psalms at least are familiar to most Christians. When life is ebbing away, or hearing is impaired, or consciousness is only partial, the sick cling to the symbols they have already known, if only to the Lord's Prayer and the 23rd Psalm. To be sure, the minister often has no little difficulty to decide with which version of the Psalms the patient is familiar, but at least he comes with the credentials of the ages rather than with some clever phraseology of his own invention.

Moreover they take both minister and patient out from the walls of the sick room or prison into the freedom of thanksgiving and praise, where self is no longer the center but God Eternal rules. And they tell of the goodness and the love of God, one hundred and twenty-seven times using the word, ordinarily translated *mercy*, which denotes his affectionate loyalty to the children he has created in his image.

Most of all, the Psalms come alive in a pastoral ministry because they are the world's best language of trust. To cite but one example from the familiar Prayer Book words:

Thy mercy, O Lord, reacheth unto the heavens,
and thy faithfulness unto the clouds.
Thy righteousness standeth like the strong mountains:
thy judgments are like the great deep . . .
How excellent is thy mercy, O God! and the children of men
shall put their trust under the shadow of thy wings . . .
They shall be satisfied with the plenteousness of thy house;
and thou shalt give them drink of thy pleasures,
as out of the river.

For with thee is the well of life;
and in thy light shall we see light. (*Ps.* 36:5-9)

It is unnecessary to collect again here the descriptions of God's character and the noblest verses expressing trust that I brought together fourteen years ago.[13] The intervening years have not impaired the value of those words, but I would put more stress now than I did then on the progression of the thought of a given psalm and relatively less on isolated verses, however glorious these may be. Similarly I would insist on the "prophetic" strain to be found in this poetry as of no less importance than the pastoral. What the Psalms say about God and history, about man's responsibility and the community, makes possible their words of comfort. And if all this is truly to come alive, it is essential that the appropriation of these Psalms should start long before the visit in the sick room.

In the days ahead, if times continue to be prosperous for a people that professes to love God but seems to the rest of the world far advanced in secularization, the Psalms may not often be much on the tongues, still less in the hearts, of the comfortable and complacent. But in every age they have not lacked singers; in every age they will enter men's hearts and come alive as men enter into them. Therefore we pray:

> O God, who has called us to sing thy praises in a strange land, if we forget thee and thy Kingdom, let our right hand wither. When in a new Bab-

ylon we are tempted to weep and hang up our harps, let the remembrance of thy holy city that was, and is, and is to come loose our tongues, and in our hearts set that Jerusalem above our highest joy, through Jesus Christ our Lord. Amen.

(*Based on Ps. 137*)

AUTHOR'S NOTES

Chapter I: The Permanence of the Psalmists' Experiences

1. Joseph Wood Krutch, *Human Nature and Human Conditions* (New York: Random House, 1959), p. 1.
2. W.J. Wolf, *The Almost Chosen People* (New York: Doubleday, 1959), p. 109.
3. William Nicholls in David M. Paton, ed., *Essays in Anglican Self-Criticism* (London: SCM Press, 1958), p. 31.
4. Cf. Ps. 73:15 RSV.
5. E. L. Mascall, *Pi in the High* (London: Faith Press, 1959), p. 11. Used with permission.
6. D.M. Baillie, *God Was in Christ* (New York: Scribner's, 1948), p. 205.
7. Possibly read "and bring you to honor"; cf. Ps. 91:15.
8. Perhaps to be read in the second person, "you."
9. If this interpretation of Ps. 82 be correct, it throws light also on the more difficult Ps. 58.
10. Cf. Ps. 30:5.
11. Milton, on December 25, 1629, after reading this psalm, appointed for Christmas Day, related it again to the coming of Christ:

    Yea, truth and justice then
    Will down return to men,
      Orbed in a rainbow; and, like glories wearing,
    Mercy will sit between
    Throned in celestial sheen,

With radiant feet the tissued clouds down steering;
And heaven, as at some festival,
Will open wide the gates of her high palace hall.
("Ode on the Morning of Christ's Nativity," stanza 15.)

12. Alec R. Vidler, *Essays in Liberality* (London: SCM Press, 1957), pp. 76-79. Used with permission.
13. M.D. Petre, *Life of George Tyrrell* (London: Longmans Green, 1912), II, 10.

Chapter II: The Psalmists' Concept of The Truth

1. Dietrich Bonhoeffer, *Prisoner for God* (New York: Macmillan, 1954), p. 165. Used with permission of *Time and Tide.*
2. Karl Jaspers, *Erneuerung der Universität.* Address at the re-opening of the Medical Faculty of the University of Heidel-berg in 1945. In *Die Wandlung,* Heidelberg, (L. Schnei-der) Vol. 1, No. 1, pp. 66ff. Used with permission.
3. *A Study of Silent Minds,* pp. 150, 133; quoted by E.W. Kemp, *The Life and Letters of Kenneth Escott Kirk* (Lon-don: Hodder & Stoughton, 1959), pp. 44f., 42. Used with permission.
4. E.B. White, *The Second Tree From the Corner* (New York: Harper, 1954), pp. 52-70. Used with permission.
5. *Ibid.,* pp. 68ff. Used with permission.
6. In Hebrew the "he" and the "we" are sharply contrasted—he is the Creator; we, the creatures.
7. For other descriptions of God cf. Pss. 23:1; 36:9; 46:1; 121:5; 91:11; 84:11; and 139:7f. See also *Munera Studiosa,* ed. by M.H. Shepherd, Jr., and S.E. Johnson (Cambridge: Episcopal Theological School, 1946), p. 18.
8. Cf. Ps. 67:2 BCP.

Chapter III: The Nature and Solution of the Psalmists' Troubles

1. Cf. Romans 3:10-12.
2. Robert Tobias, *Communist-Christian Encounter in East Europe*

(Indianapolis: School of Religion Press, 1956), pp. 207, 205. Used with permission.

3. William Nicholls, "On Living in the Twentieth Century" in D.M. Paton, ed., *Essays in Anglican Self-Criticism* (London: SCM Press, 1958), pp. 30f. Used with permission.
4. No modern translation, however accurate, quite takes the place of the Prayer Book's "gat me to my Lord right humbly."
5. For the interpretation of this passage cf. Sheldon H. Blank, "The Nearness of God and Psalm Seventy-Three" in *To Do and To Teach* (Lexington, Kentucky: The College of the Bible, 1953).
6. M.J.M. Paton, "Can We Ignore the Establishment?" in D.M. Paton, ed., *op. cit.*, pp. 139-140. Used with permission.
7. Quoted E.W. Kemp, *op. cit.*, p. 208.
8. I.e., to the east or west.
9. I.e., conceals nothing from thee.
10. *Laws*, X, 905.
11. *Confessions*, V, II.

Chapter IV: Poetry in an Age of Prose

1. A definition familiar to older graduates of Williams College, who were students of the late A.H. Licklider.
2. *Atlantic Monthly*, December 1953, p. 26.
3. Ps. 24:3. Many scholars think three accents; see the following note.
4. Ps. 23:6. Ordinarily it is assumed that this rhythm in which the second half-line is shorter than the first—the so-called elegiac or *qinah* meter—uses three accents followed by two. More probably it should be read as four followed by three. The reason is twofold. On the one hand, it is possible to read some of the lines with no less than four and three stresses. The tongue does not easily and normally manage more than three or at most four syllables with only one accent. That is why words like "inestimable" and "despicable" are not easy to pronounce, and why Americans make "labórat(o)ry" into "láboratóry" with two accents, and

why the Englishman's conclusion to "Deuteronomy" is so indistinct. On the other hand, one beauty of poetry is that it introduces accents into lines which would lack them in prose. "When shall we three meet again?" In prose these six words bear no more than three accents. But put them with other words "In thunder, lightning, or in rain?" Notice that the word "or" now bears one. And continue,

> "Where's the place, upon the heath,
> There to meet with Macbeth."

All this is verse, not prose, because four accents are measured regularly against other four. In Hebrew, as in English, what looks like 3:3 meter is usually 4:4, and what is commonly considered 3:2 is more likely 4:3. Of course, if those scholars were right who see a change in meter from line to line, various ways of reading Hebrew poetry are possible, but regularity of rhythm is essential, not optional, so that it is preferable to give even such a short half-line as that at the end of the 23rd Psalm three accents, rather than to compress other lines of this psalm into 3 and 2.

5. E.g., Pss. 1, 15, 79, 119.
6. E.g., Pss. 38:13f., 124:4f., 131:2, 137:3, 16:11.
7. E.g., Pss. 46:4 (streams).
8. E.g., in Ps. 91, parts of vv. 4, 7, 15.
9. E.g., Ps. 65:1; cf. the difference between Hebrew and Greek.
10. E.g., Ps. 16:4.
11. E.g., the conclusions of Pss. 96 and 98.
12. Cf. Ps. 49:14, 73:24, and the Greek of Ps. 16:10.
13. For the meaning of the Hebrew verb in this line, see Proverbs 25:24 (21:9).
14. The following psalms may originally have been of the length indicated:
    10 lines: 6, 20, 23, 47, 64, 65, 96, 97, 98
    20 lines: 29, 49, 50, 51, 72, 80, 88, 99, 116, 132
    30 lines: 31, 42-43, 68, 118
    40 lines: 45, 104, 105, 106
    50 lines: 18, 89

70 lines: 78
22 or a multiple of 22: 9-10, 25, 33, 34, 37, 94, 103, 111, 112, 119, 145
8 lines: 1, 3, 4, 8, 11, 12, 16, 19A, 40B-70, 54, 56, 57, 60, 61, 64, 67, 75, 76, 82, 108, 113, 114, 120, 121, 122, 124, 125, 126, 127, 128, 129, 130, 137, 138, 141, 144, 149
12 lines: 2, 14/53, 21, 24B, 26, 28, 30, 36, 39, 41, 46, 52, 59, 63, 93, 140, 142
16 lines: 5, 17, 40A, 48, 77, 84, 143.

15. The refrain is found in the 9th-10th, 19th-20th, and 29th-30th lines of the poem. The additions are vs. 4a (Hebrew 5a), "Let me make my memorial offering and an oblation," and vs. 8 (Hebrew 9), which contradicts the gloomy verse preceding by declaring, "By day the Lord commands his devotion and at night his song is with me, a prayer to the god of my life."
16. Ps. 25:22. This verse is outside the alphabetical scheme which characterizes the first 21 verses of this psalm.
17. Ps. 96:13. Cf. Ps. 98:9.
18. Cf. also Ps. 36:5ff.
19. As reported by Dwight Macdonald in the *New Yorker*, Nov. 14, 1953, p. 205. Used with permission.
20. *Ibid.*, p. 203.
21. *Ibid.*, p. 196.
22. E.g., Pss. 40:5; 119:147; 139:15; 4:2; also 5:6; 55:15; 31:8; 22:17; 66:12; 7:9.
23. E.g., with the help of the ancient version, cf. Pss. 49:11; 85:8; 145:13; or of conjectural emendations, cf. Pss. 91:9; 107:17; 2:11f; 32:6; 73:10.
24. E.g., Pss. 42:2; 126:1; 127:2.
25. Barzun, *op. cit.*, p. 28.
26. E.g., For "my soul longs, yea, faints," why not "I faint with longing"? Would it not be well to remove the proper name, *Baca,* and perhaps read "to stand on the threshold in the house of my God"?
27. Cf. Pss. 98:1, 2; 20:5, 6; 21:5; 33:17.
28. Ps. 23:4. Cf. Pss. 15:3; 121:7, etc.
29. Cf. Ps. 34:20—"he keeps all his bones."

Chapter V: Coming Alive Today

1. The hymn was probably the second part of the hallel, Pss. 113-118.
2. Paul S. Minear, ed., *The Nature of the Unity We Seek* (St. Louis: The Bethany Press, 1958), p. 113.
3. C.S. Lewis, *Reflections on the Psalms* (New York: Harcourt, Brace, 1958), pp. 20-33.
4. F.A. Iremonger, *William Temple* (London: Oxford University Press, 1948), p. 514f. For testimony to Ps. 145, see D.M. Baillie, *Theology of the Sacraments* (New York: Scribner's, 1957), p. 35.
5. Pp. 29; 338f.
6. Cf. pp. 56-60.
7. Or, "uttering slanders against me" (RSV).
8. Adelaide Teague Case, *Seven Psalms* (Woman's Press, 1935).
9. Quoted Paton and Martin, *Paragraphs for Sundays and Holy Days* (London: SCM Press, 1957). Used with permission.
10. P. 88.
11. *Omnium existentium opifex Domine, statue pedes nostros in atriis tuis, & aedifica Ierusalem supernam in nobis, fiat pax continua in virtute tua, ut & eiusdem semper civitatis bona devoti quaeramus, & te praestante inveniamus.*
12. Quoted by Dr. Case in *op. cit.*, p. 37.
13. *Munera Studiosa*, ed. by M.H. Shepherd, Jr., and S.E. Johnson (Cambridge: Episcopal Theological School, 1946), pp. 18-21.

INDEX OF SCRIPTURAL REFERENCES

The Psalms (*continued*)